THE BIG BOOK

ON

DISSOCIATE IDENTITY DISORDER

ITS CAUSES AND CURE

Book One of a Two Book Set

BOOK TWO IN THE: "CONTENDING FOR THE FAITH SERIES"

By

Dr. Tom Knotts, Jr.

www.SRA-DIDFreedomInChrist.com

Foreword

Dissociative Identity Disorder (DID), as defined by the American Psychiatric Association's Diagnostic and Statistical Manual of Mental Disorders, is a mental condition whereby a single individual evidences two or more distinct identities or personalities, each with its own pattern of perceiving and interacting with the environment. The presumption is that at least two personalities may routinely take control of the individual's behavior.

The American Psychiatric Association would never dream of the possibility of a spiritual realm that is beyond human sight. They would never think it possible for a demon or demons to possess and control an individual. In their view the spiritual world is not reality. They will always treat physical symptoms with what they accept as reality or with medication of some sort.

Tom Knotts does a tremendous job in helping us understand both the reality of a spiritual world and the reality of Spiritual Warfare. Dr. Knotts helps educate us on the many schemes of our enemy, "Satan." While the secular world deals with the physical we as Christians must deal with the spiritual. Demon possession is real. The spiritual world is a reality. This book is a must read for every Christian Counselor who believes in the reality of the Occult and wishes to see Jesus set the captive free. Jesus says, "I am the Way the Truth and the Life." He goes on to say, "You shall know the truth and the truth shall set you free." Only those who truly know the truth can assist those who need to be set free by the truth.

Dr. Mark Crook

Dean of Psychology and Christian Counseling

Louisiana Baptist University

Forward

    I have broken The Big Book of Dissociate Identity Disorder into two separate volumes. The first book is designed to familiarize the reader with the disorder in order to give them a better understanding of the various tenets of the disorder. The second volume is intended to educate the counselor on the internal workings of the psyche and how the disorder occurs and develops, to include all the mechanics and operatives within the various levels of the conscious. There are many different intricacies of problems that accompany dissociation thus making it a challenging field to understand. It has been my purpose to thoroughly explore the fabric, of the inner workings of the identity and how it meshes together to create the many different paradigms of dissociation disorder.

TABLE OF CONTENTS

Chapter:

> As the abundance of sin increases, the hearts of many are growing colder, those in the field of counseling need to prepare themselves for the generational wave of victims that are already surfacing in our nation today; I'm referring to those suffering from Dissociate Identity Disorder.

11. Conclusion: "Considerations for the Counselor"

    a. The Question of Calling

    b. Preparedness

    c. Time Allocations

    d. Dangers and Pitfalls

    e. Personal Time

    f. Friends, Colleges and Accountability

    g. When Enough is Enough

    h. Passing the Torch

Prologue:

As the abundance of sin increases, the hearts of many are growing colder, those in the field of counseling need to prepare themselves for the generational wave of victims that are already surfacing in this nation today; I'm referring to those suffering from Dissociate Identity Disorder. Violence and crime have risen to epidemic portions in many areas of these United States. Crimes against children, both physically and sexually are so common, they no longer have effect on the nation as they once had. It is reported that two out of every five girls will be molested, physically and/or sexually assaulted, by a friend or family member, prior to the age of sixteen. The statistics say the same will happen to one out of every six boys. Our nation has become so de-sensitized to the atrocities plaguing its inhabitants, that the dysfunctional family unit has now become the common family unit. We have reformed our school and state family systems to accommodate these malignant strains, since prevention is no longer an option. Stress and pressures upon single parent homes where there is no father figure, coupled with financial inabilities to provide the mere basic necessities, have created environments where our nation's greatest heritage, it's youth, no longer have the safe nurturing environment needed for proper self development. As a result, we are in the midst of a second generation of teens and adolescents suffering, from a myriad of anti-social ills and deficits. Of these conditions, one that has risen to the for-front is Dissociate Identity Disorder.

Dissociate Identity Disorder is often referred to in its abbreviated state as DID. DID is a ***hyper-synchronization*** process that happens within the brain, when the person is placed into a situation, where the need to survive is challenged. When a child is placed under duress, trauma, or conditions of extreme neglect, the brain will dissociate the child, from the situation. It is a coping self defense mechanism, where the brain makes tolerable, that which would otherwise be unbearable. Dissociation is a disorder that affects all aspects of the persons psyche. It is the psyche that dictates, governs and controls all areas of the individual's life. At the rate that violence, crime and neglect are increasing in this country, DID will be one of the leading, treatable mental abnormalities of this next generation.

Dissociate Identity Disorder is a treatable condition. Through faith in Jesus Christ, a person's alters can receive healing and then be integrated back into the core life essence of the psyche. The key to helping the individual with DID, is being able to pull the alternate personalities to the front of the conscious and then leading them to an understanding of what it is that has caused the dissociation. It is the act of acknowledge the truth of what has happened to them and then leading them in the act of forgiving the one who has hurt them, that enables them to release the negative energy, bitterness, anger, depression, hatred, and so on. This internalized pain is the wedge that maintains the splitting of the psyche. Catharsis happens through the act of forgiveness; forgiving the person who has hurt them and receiving forgiveness for their own sins through the Lord Jesus Christ. Because DID has become so wide spread, those in the field of counseling, are going to be confronted with the disorder. It is essential that the counselor be able to identify the disorder and then be able to treat it effectively. I have spoken to more than one counselor that has expressed concern over their inability to help their clients that have DID. They tell me that this is not an area that they want to be counseling in, they would prefer to do marriage counseling or some other type of counseling for which they are trained, but they are being flooded with victims and survivors that are in desperate need for someone, anyone, who understands their condition and that can properly help them. For this reason, the counselor needs to be equipped, not only to recognize DID, but also to understand the intricacies involved with the disorder so they can offer better treatment to the client.

The purpose of this book is to aid those who work in the counseling field by equipping them to identify the characteristics and symptoms of DID and then to aid the client in the healing process. As you read this book, you will find there are many areas of deliberate repetition and redundancy. The reasoning behind this is to offer as many opportunities as possible, to the reader for a better understanding of the nature of the disorder. The case scenarios in this book are real and have been used with permission, for illustrative purposes, to aid in the understanding process and also, for clarifying the characteristic diversity found in the many facets of DID. The names and places have been changed or withheld to protect the identity of those involved.

Inside the reading, there are terms that you may be unfamiliar with, such as, survivor. Those suffering from extreme dissociate conditions are often referred to as, *"survivors."* The reason is simple; as with any extreme tragedy, there will be those who have survived. The survivor is the one, who against all odds, has come through the terrible ordeal, victorious, and is now seeking healing and restoration.

Working with DID is not for the timid. This work is very taxing on the counselor and cannot be accomplished in the strength of man.[1] It is here that we must call upon the Great Physician, the Lord Jesus Christ, and ask Him to intercede on behalf of the individual. It is my position that only God can make straight that which is crooked and bring the healing that is so desperately needed in these people's lives.[2] It is for this reason that the methodology proposed is Nouthetic; [3] for which no apologies are made. There are over two hundred philosophies on counseling. Each counselor must choose how they will conduct their own personal ministry, gleaning where possible and learning new techniques, to be the best in their respected field. My personal philosophy and conviction is that the Scriptures are the infallible Word of God and are good for all aspects of life and living.[4] I also stand on the premise that God is God, and He alone can bring wholeness and happiness into the lives of mankind.[5] Without the indwelling of the Holy Spirit, we are not complete.[6] In fact, there will always be something missing from a person's life until they accept Jesus Christ as their personal Savior.

_____

[1] The Holy Bible: Zechariah 4:6
[2] Ecclesiastes 1:15
[3] Nouthetic is Bible Based Counseling
[4] 2 Timothy 3:16
[5] 1 Samuel 2:2; Isaiah 45:6, 21; Ezekiel 29:16
[6] Colossians 2:10

For complete healing to be achieved, it is imperative that we seek to lead the client in a way that develops a personal relationship with the Lord Jesus Christ. We must seek complete healing for the individual and that includes the body, mind, soul and spirit. It is my prayer that both counselor and counselee will experience the fullness of Christ. May the Lord richly bless and keep you in His will as you endeavor to serve Him.

In Christ's love: Dr. Tom Knotts, Jr.

WWW.SRA-DIDFreedomInChrist.com

I would like to dedicate this book to the memory of my father; Tom Knotts, Sr. The son of Rance and Myrtle Knotts of Timmonsville, South Carolina. My father always believed in me and asked me many times to put my work into writing for others to share. Thanks Dad, I will see you in heaven some day.

The Definition of Dissociative Identity Disorder

As they brought the individual into the room I noticed how physically developed he was. Though only about five foot two inches tall, his weight was easily over two hundred and thirty pounds, all of which was solid muscle. The correctional officers brought him in wearing leg shackles, a straightjacket and a helmet. It was obvious by the way they stood holding him firmly by both of his arms, that in spite of his restraints, they considered him to be a very dangerous person; and they were not taking any chances. Under these conditions, I did not feel that the man would speak freely so I asked the officers to remove the helmet from his head and to allow him to sit down across the table from me, after which, they could wait outside the door until I was done. They immediately expressed concern for my safety but I told them that if I had any problems they were just outside the door and could easily rush in. They looked at each other and asked me if I knew what I was doing; I assured them that I did. They sat him down and told him to stay put, before they walked out.

What I saw gave me no inclination that this person was in any way violent or dangerous. His demeanor was warm and friendly. The man warmly smiled as I asked him his name and why he was in this facility. He told me that he honestly did not know. He said that he had woken up, sitting in a pile of glass in front of a store just as the police arrived. They arrested and charged him with breaking and entering, and burglary. He told me he did not know how he could have gotten there. He believed that someone must have knocked him out and put the stolen merchandise in his hands, before leaving.

NOTE: It is common for alternate personalities to experience states of fugue. Fugue, is a condition where the presenting alter[7] goes into a type of hibernation and is replaced by another alter. While the personality is in fugue, time stops for them. It is common, that while they are in the fugue state, for the brain to run a script to explain any losses in time they may experience. A script is a prepared explanation, that the alter will believe when it comes back to the conscious level of the mind. Just like in a play performance, each actor will have their own role to perform in the story, from a script that has been written just for that character. In DID each alter will have pre-written scripts that are stored in the unconscious part of the brain. These scripts are played out when they are moved in and out of the active conscious. The presenting alter is personality that is in the active conscious. When a person experiences a fugue episode, they will be replaced by another alter, that will come to the surface of the conscious to perform the role for which it is designed. When its act is over it will then go back into storage, being replaced by another alter, until it is needed again. When this happens, the person is unaware of everything that has transpired while they were in the fugue state. All time stops while in fugue.

---

[7] Alter is a term used to describe an alternate personality. In a dissociate, there can be as little as a few to several hundred different alters.

During this period of time, I was involved in the prison ministry, as director over the Midwest region of the state in which I lived. My responsibilities included overseeing a number of chaplains in various facilities, spread across the state. The head of the facility, where the man was housed, had asked me to come to work with him. They were hoping I could calm him down and also discover what was causing his extreme character swings. After the initial introductions were out of the way I began to ask a serious of non-related questions. This is a technique I use to try and trigger a person; it helps me to be able to identity root issues or problems within the inner psyche. I watch for facial and body expressions with a particular interest on the pupil and iris of the eye. I began the questioning to try and discover what was causing this man's unpredictable behavior; that was when everything changed. The man sitting across the table from me disappeared and was replaced by another man; a potentially dangerous man appeared. I watched as he triggered,[8] something I've seen many times in those with Dissociative conditions. As the new alter emerged, his eyes flickered up and down for a few moments and when they stopped a cold, dead stare was locked onto me. No longer was John Doe, the warm and politely confused inmate in front of me; here was an emotionless, machine positioned across the table from me in simple restraints. I began to feel sick inside! I was now kicking myself inside for sending the officers outside. I

---

[8] Triggering is a term used to describe the changing of alters that is initiated by stimulus. The stimulus can be either internal or externally motivated. It comes from the reference to how a gun is fired by the pulling of the trigger.

knew that if I did not do something very quickly that I was going to be in serious trouble.

I had been working in the correctional system for over six years as a chaplain. I was also on staff of a large Christian Ministry as a trainer and instructor, for the placement of chaplains into state and county facilities. I had seen, this same dead stare, many times before in the eyes of psychopaths and murderers. Here were those same eyes again, and they were looking through me. I knew he was sizing me up. He crouched down in his chair with his eyes just above the table. He was positioning himself to knock the table into me, and even though he was restrained, I knew he was going to attack me! I said in a slow and quite voice, "Hi what's your name? I'm Pastor Tom; it's nice to meet you." The man shook his head slowly from side to side and in a strong southern voice responded, "You're not going to hurt John!" I replied, "I wouldn't hurt John, he's my friend, I'm here to see if I can help him, maybe you can help me do this. "Who are you," he replied. "I know you're not going to hurt him, I'll see to that." At this point the man looked very powerful and confident in his abilities to defend this body. He showed absolutely no indication of fear, but rather a black and white pattern of thinking had emerged. This is a common characteristic of purpose driven alternate personalities with inner psyche defined roles. The alternate personality in front of me was a defender. Its job was to remove anyone or anything that may seek to hurt John Doe; who was the main alter.[9] I found out later from the guards that this man would do 1,200 pushups every

---

[9] Alter is the abbreviation for alternate personality

morning and 1,000 sit ups before breakfast.[10] He definitely had the ability to protect himself.

What ensued, over the next two and a half hours, was a very intense and sobering counseling session. I met with over a dozen of this man's alters in that short time period, ranging in ages from five years old to some in their early thirties. I began working through the several presenting alters, categorizing them according to age and role and then I developed, a safe internal environment, in which to house the various alters. I placed a two story house into his mind and extracted the alters from where they were located in the several layers of John's psyche. There were several reasons for doing this:

a) The alternate personalities would be aware of each others presence
b) They would feel safer being together
c) Having them organized together made it easier to access them for later work in healing and integration

This individual was a complex dissociate that resulted from being an SRA-DID, with high level programming and a multi-faceted alter system.[11]

---

[10] A alter will become the best at whatever its job is. As defender this person's alter would work out to the extreme. He was also very skilled in boxing and the martial arts.

[11] SRA-DID stand for Satanic Ritual Abuse-Dissociate Identity Disorder. In this type of abuse alters are intentionally split from the main psyche and then programmed through trauma, hypnotism and conditioning. They are completely obedient to their owner/programmer and will do any job for which they are created.

Dissociation if often hard to discern because it has so many varying degrees. If you were to look at it in the form of a line graph it would go from simple fragmentation of memories and personality to the designed intellect, which has fully developed personalities that are usually unaware of anyone but themselves in the persons mind. The various types of alters from fragmentation to complete will be discussed in greater detail in chapter five.

I have broken the degrees of dissociation into four categories.

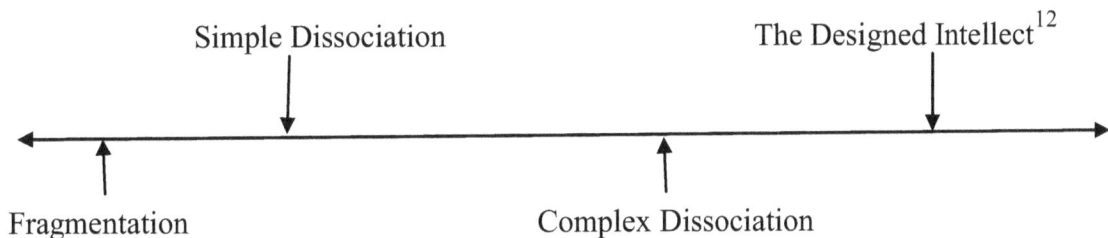

Simple Dissociation   The Designed Intellect[12]

Fragmentation   Complex Dissociation

The Designed intellect at first appearance would seem to be quite different from the fragment but actually they are very similar in construct, stemming from the same bio-genetic foundation. The fragment is easier to deal with since it is usually a composition of body or sensory memories without a fully formalized intellect, whereas, the designed intellect has its own personality, desires and ambitions. Dissociation is not a breakdown of the mental facilities. Disassociation Identity Disorder is a *hyper synchronization* within the psyche of an individual for the purpose of enabling them to, not only survive what would be an otherwise unbearable situation, while continuing

---

[12] The designed intellect happens when a person's mind is intentionally split for the purpose of mind control programming

living and developing within the parameters of the social constraint in which they dwell. Often this environment is a hostile world, filled with chaos and turmoil. Rather than having a home life with set parameters, the boundaries within the home are blurred, leaving the individual with a never ending uncertainty of what may happen next. This constant presence of uncertainty creates an overload of stress and anxiety that the child's mind is ill equipped to deal with. So what are they to do? Catharsis is not an option as the child is often afraid to reveal the secrets of an abusive situation. The brain of the child needs to eliminate stress from the active conscious; it finds relief through dissociation.

To dissociate means, "To break the connection between."[13] The mind breaks the connection between the event or action and the child's conscious, enabling the child to live a life where their minds believe that their psychological needs are being met. The mind disassociates the trauma from the conscious and places it into a memory holding module. The memory holding module is the actual alter that is created. It can be an alter that is a fragment where body and sensory memories associated with the trauma are stored or it can be a complete alter that is created. A complete alter is formed through repetitive acts against the mind of the child or through long, drawn out periods of duress, such as torture. The alter is the storage point for the memories associated with the event that caused the dissociation. If the act that caused the dissociation reoccurs, the brain will have a neurological pathway already established for dealing with the trauma and will

---

[13] Webster's New World Dictionary of the American Language, pg. 179

automatically take the same neural route for modeling the event and the memories associated with it. The depth and intensity of the sensory input of the trauma will be the determining factor in how well developed the alter will become. If the act is drawn out for a long period of time or is repetitive than the brain will create a complete alter with its own personal identity to deal with the situation. The complete alter will have a black and white thinking pattern with a defined role. It will know its job and will perform that job to the best of its ability. Once the neural pathway is established, the next time the trauma occurs, the brain will instantly bring the created alter to the surface to deal with the situation. The presenting alter will be in fugue until the act is over. Only after the duress is complete will the presenting alter be returned back to the active conscious where a preplanned script will ensure that the presenting alter remains unaware of what has occurred. A script is a logical train of thought that the brain produces to explain any loss of time or anything that may reveal actions that the presenting alter are not a part of. The presenting alter will be that alternate personality that is at the front of the conscious. The presenting alter will change according to need and survival. A alter that is a escort will be at the front when she is with a client while the alter that works in the shopping center will be the presenter when at the shopping center. Each personality will have its own clearly defined role. The script keeps them safely hidden from each other and those that are not to know of their presence. They need this anonymity; with everything in its proper place the brain will not be stressed. The internal pressures from value and belief systems being challenged, is nullified. This is why you can have a satanic priestess and a lady who teaches Sunday school to children in her church in the same body. They do not know about each other. They are true to their values and beliefs so there is no inner tension or turmoil. Each alter stays true to its role. The black and white thinking pattern leaves no area of grey, the various alters will stay pure in their design, use and role.

Here is a governing rule of dissociation: The more intense the abuse or trauma, the greater the depth of seperative formation that will occur in the split of the psyche. In other words a complete alter can instantly be formed from something that is incredibly traumatic. Situations like near death experiences, being raped, tortured, severely abused, or any other extremely traumatic experience can result in the instant creation of a completely developed alter. In cases of extreme neglect the mind can also create, co-existing, complete alters, for social interactions with the presenting alter. Companionship is a basic social life need. The brain will create an alternate personality to keep the person from completely withdrawing and shutting down. This basic life need is met by giving the psyche a release mechanism; in this case, a socially accepted partner that desires to spend time with them, valuing them, and accepting them just as they are.

I have worked with many clients that have had several alters created from neglect. When the time came to bring these alters to healing and integration the main person was greatly saddened at the thought of losing their best, and in some cases, their only friends. Sometimes, because of the fear of loneliness, they will refuse to allow the co-existing alter to be integrated. Realize a person that has lived separated from others will never have developed the social skill necessary to acquire relationships or friends. To them it is a very fearful thing. It is easier and often preferred to just disassociate from the fear and for the brain to revert back, creating an alternate personality with which they can relate. If a person has alters created from neglect it is very common for them to resist integration of the alters. What happens in these cases is that the brain will place the alter back into its storage module for safe keeping. Many children will create alternate personalities by fantasizing. When the neglect ends these co-existing alters will be stored for later use. For complete healing the person must be taught how to face the world without disassociating or withdrawing from society. The struggle with this is that; once the brain has learned to dissociate from problems, rather than face the issue at hand, disassociation will become the primary means that the brain uses to deal with intolerable or stressful situations.

DID is a condition that was formerly known as Multiple Personality Disorder or MPD. Due to advancements in understanding about the condition, it was re-defined as Dissociate Identity Disorder. This is because it technically is not multiple personalities but rather an identity disorder that is created through disassociation. It is the same person but in varying degrees and combinations of the:

1) Intellect
2) Will

3) Emotion

4) Mind

5) Intelligence

6) Body

7) Memories

DID is a fascinating condition that is often masked with an abundance of presenting symptoms. Because of this, the dissociate is often misdiagnosed an average of seven times before being recognized as a disassociate. The primary reason for this is, when they are asked what is bothering them, they will give symptoms for PTSD,[14] Anxiety Disorders, Bipolar, Schizophrenia, sleeping disorders or some other problem. What needs to be understood when working with a disassociate is that, you are not diagnosing a single person, there are usually many alters within the person all of which will have different problems. These problematic conditions are not the main problem they are like the leaves on a tree. They are called *the presenting problem.* This is the problem that the person comes to you for but it is not the real source of internal conflict. The genesis will be found in the original insult to the brain, which caused a separation in the conscious. That is the root of the problem. The presenting problem is only the external symptom of the incongruity of the lower conscious. The root will have to be dealt with in order to eradicate the leaves.

---

[14] Post traumatic stress disorder

True healing will come when all of the alters have been brought to healing and integrated back into the life essence. I use the term life essence rather than core because a child in the formation stages of life will not have an established identity. They will not have a core identity from which the other alters have been split. While in the formative stages of life, it is the life essence that is split. The life essence is the effulgence of life energy from the brain stem. Disassociates will have a splitting that occurs at the base of the no-conscious part of the brain allowing for prompting the development of several different identities. True healing will come when all of the alters have been brought to healing and then integrated into the life essence so there is only one mind, heart, soul, spirit, will and intellect.

When working with the associate remember that each of the alters are actually the person. They just have been allocated to specific roles and tasks that each has their own value and belief system. They have been separated to remove conflict from the brain. The brain can be illustrated as the computer which houses all of the various software programs, using them to the best of their capabilities and function with as little conflict as possible. The brain creates separate identities to meet the demands of differing value and belief systems. They grow up alongside one another, developing and maturing into their own person all the while of being unaware of each other. I remember a client that told me that they would witness to others of Christ but there was an individual that had confronted her saying that she needed to live for Christ if she was going to tell others about him. What the Christian did not know is that she had an alternate personality that was being used as a prostitute for groups of men and bestiality. This part had been severally abused and had been used her whole life as a prostitute by her father. In order to deal with the trauma her brain had separated and created multiple identities that grew and matured alongside each other, but completely ignorant of each other's existence. Each alter will have to be individually dealt with. They will have their own:

a) Personal Identity

    a. Who they believe themselves to be

    b. What they believe others believe about them

    c. Their own beliefs about God

    d. Their own value systems

        i. What is important in life

        ii. What acts are right for them to perform

        iii. How they are to be treated by others

        iv. How they are to treat and respond to others

        v. What love is: many times they have been conditioned to believe that pain is love. They only feel desired when they are being abused, hurt or used by others.

    e. Their own philosophy of life

    f. Their own particular role they play in the individual

    g. Their own private set of memories

    h. Their own set of definitions of terms and words

i. Their own personal self image

j. They will also have their own personal reason for being created by the brain. Here is an example drawn from a client I worked with.

    i. An animal alter for bestiality: it was created because she was being forced to have sex with an animal. She was told she was nothing but an animal so her brain created an animal alter.

    ii. A analyst: She was told that she would work in a certain job and in order to do that job, the brain created an alter that was purely an analyst.

    iii. A dominatrix: This part was created to serve all sexual fetishes by those she was assigned to be an escort to.

    iv. A wife and a mother: She was told that she was to begin having a family so that she would produce the next set of slaves for her owner. Like an animal breeder, these abuser/programmers will make slaves out of their own child and then will do the same to their grandchildren. When the woman got in her mid thirties it was decided that she would get married and have children. Her spouse was even picked out for her. He continued to use her for the family as a sexual slave as that was part of the agreement for marrying her.

v. Active Christian Church Member: She was to have a front that would appear to be very dedicated to God and the church as part of the front she would present.

This is something very disturbing to read about and frankly many that read this will not believe it but the slave trafficking business has been happening for centuries and it is still very active today. I have worked with people who were considered to be property. I have even confronted their *owners*. The use of hypnotism on sexual alters is a common and widespread practice. Once again in the formative stages of life an alter that is created and developed will have its own identity. If you do not understand that each alter is independent than working with someone with the disorder will seem complex and often overwhelming. Do not become focused upon the many facets of the person. I will state it again; If you can understand this one truth your job as a counselor will be much easier: DID is not many persons but rather it is a multi-faceting of a single personality.

Since we live in an age of computers one of the best ways to illustrate dissociate identity disorder would be to compare it with an operating system on a computer.

> You have the computer body which is the housing unit holding all of the parts of the computer. This represents the person's body

> You have a hard drive which contains all of the filing and allocating systems, with set parameters and memory modeling units. This represents the brain

> You have the memory which composes the information stored in the hard drive. This memory has an active memory that is constantly being brought to the surface for active use and then placed back into the hard drive where it goes into a dormant state. The memory is selective; only the memories associated with particular files, systems or programs will come to the surface. This represents that alters of the dissociate. Each will have its own personal memories allocated to it alone. When not in use they go into a dormant state of fugue.

> In the hard drive are the software programs which compose the operating systems that control how the hard drive and memory interface with the user. This represents the mind of the individual. Each will have partitions created to they only activate with proper allocation of assignment. Roles are defined and kept indigenous to the alter of origin.

The human brain is the most complex and advances computer ont he planet. One human brain has more capacity and ability than every computer on the world put together. The brain is also a functioning organ that's primary purpose is existence. It is designed to operate the body and mind in a way that ensures perpetuity of life with an increasing potential of quality and a desire to thrive. When you look at a computer you may only see a word based program running but what you do not see are the many programs that are part of the operating system which enable the word processing program to run efficiently. In fact you can have several hundred programs all running simultaneously. Though they each have separate functions and independent roles; they work together to create a symbiotic whole. The brain and mind of a dissociate work together; with each alter having a specific function and role that they perform. There will be some alters that seem insignificant; but they are not. The brains response is that it only creates that which is necessary. If there were created it is because they are necessary. They have a purpose for their existence. I want to emphasize this point again: No matter how insignificant an alter appears to be, it would not have been created by the brain without a prominent part in the collective whole.

The person, John Doe that I had worked with in the prison facility began life as a single facet life essence. He had no alters or conscious splits. He was a single, whole conscious. Because of extreme trauma that began early in his childhood, the true person, which was a single whole conscious at birth, was split. Those *splits* because of the extreme abuse they endured were further poly-fragmented. These fragments developed and matured until they became over a dozen separate alternate personalities. Each of these alters had their own independent role and function with varying levels of conscious awareness. Another unique aspect of the alters is that they have their own personal reason for existing; in other words they were created to meet a very specific need. It is the need that determines their prominence and role capacity. At least three of the dozen alters were primary alters.[15]For instance the protector was created to keep him from being hurt while in prison. It began exercising several times a day until it could do 1200 pushups and then 1000 sit ups without stopping. Primaries hold a prominent role in the person's life.

John's mind had split so that he could survive a very traumatic event. These splits were initiated by the survival coping mechanism housed in the no-conscious layer of the brain. A survival coping mechanism is a psycho-autonomic response to a life and death situation. Within the biogenetic blueprint of the brain there is a built in primal drive to live. The body and brain seek above all things to exist. The optimum desire is for the ability to thrive and prosper while existing. There arc several things that a person needs in order to survive.

Survival is not limited to bodily needs but includes the facilitating of a mind that can function and interact within the social environment that the individual is a part of. The brain forms what is called the personal identity in order to meet these developing needs while reaching its ultimate goal; living and thriving in a positive environment, where the person is wanted, accepted and desired. Alters that are created through abuse will find the role of being

---

[15] A primary alter is one that is at the front for a majority of time. For instance they may hold a job for the person, or be they play the role of the married spouse. A primary holds a significant role.

used and abused as their positive environment. They will have a reversal of good for evil, hate for love, pain for pleasure. It will be diametrically opposite to what is considered normal and proper. This is because they have been created to do their best in the negative situation. If that means the ability to please their abuser, than they will become the best they can at receiving abuse. This ensures their survival and ability to thrive and live in what they consider to be a positive environment.

The mind and the body both have needs that must be met if they are to develop properly. If a person is placed into a situation that causes great conflict, to the minds ability to cope and/or threatens the body's existence, than the brain will work out a survival strategy. **It will do what it has to in order to survive.** This is how the brain develops the coping survival mechanism to work. Because the victim does plan the traumatic events their brain is forced to make spur decisions that the undeveloped mind is not equipped to deal with. In these cases the brain will dissociate the active conscious from the event. It will then create another personality that is molded by the event so that its existence based solely for dealing with that specific type of trauma or event. Because disassociation happens to a child prior to the age of seven fighting back is not an option. A child cannot stop an adult from hurting them. Their only change on survival is to adapt to the situation. This adaptation takes the form of dissociation. An alternate personality is then created that will deal with the trauma. The brain will work to detach it from the body and emotions and conscious mind. It will work primarily from the rear of the brain where the fight and flight center is located. Whenever the trauma is repeated the active conscious will be shut down by being put into a state of fugue giving the active conscious over to the alternate personality that has been designed to deal with the abuse. The alter will perform its function and role. When the abuse is over the alternate personality is placed back into the unconscious, where it, and all of the bad memories will be kept and stored. The alternate personality and all of its memories will be kept separated from the active conscious. This allows the person to live two very different lives; one where they are abused and the other where they interact with society, with no appearance of anything being wrong. They will appear very normal. This is because part of their ability to survive is tied with their ability to fit into public without bringing attention to themselves or their abusers. The fear of further being hurt by the abuser if the victim ever tells on them forces the brain to keep the active presenting alter ignorant of any of the abuse. The life they live in the public will appear to be normal. The brain will try to keep the presenting alter busy and focused on other things so that it does not have the ability to learn of the other alter and what it is enduring. There is a developmental sequence that occurs in the formation of the personal identity.

When a child is in the early developmental stages of life, their mental development will be halted and then restructured to accommodate a life threatening experience. This could be in the form of great fear, pain, trauma, abuse or neglect. For instance, an infant or toddler that is deprived of human touch will disassociate from the lack of this basic life need. Neglect causes dissociation in children! The body and mind have different needs that must be met if they are to develop properly. A person's identity is formed by physical and perceptional stimulation they receive, or the lack thereof, during the first seven years of life. As the brain grows so will the layers of the mind that form the personal identity.

A simple definition of Identity is how a person views them self. It is what they see when they look in the mirror. The self image of a disassociate is often distorted so it is what they *believe* to be true about themselves. Remember the identity of the alters can greatly vary. The alters identities have been created to meet specific needs. The mind will perceive, **what it needs to believe to be true,** for the alter to carry out its role. What their mind perceives about them, may or may not be the true image, of who they really are. Here are two examples of alters with distorted identity perceptions. These are from three cases that I worked with.

Multiple Identities will have their own unique self perception

I had a middle aged lady referred to me for counseling. The counselor that referred her to me said that he believed that the woman was a schizophrenic but that there was too much that did not fit into the pattern. I met with the client and asked her why I was seeing her; why she had come to see me. She said that someone was coming into her home and leaving things in her home so she would know they were they and also bringing in strange food items and even eating out of her food items. Because she feared that someone may be poisoning her she had begun putting tape on the lids of the food and if it was disturbed she would throw away the entire container. I asked her what items were being left in the home and she told me that she would get up in the morning and there would be men's clothing and shoes in her closet. She would find this about once or twice a month. She said the police did not believe her because they could find no evidence of a break in. They had even taken finger prints and only found hers in the apartment. She said that she was not crazy but the fear was driving her that way. I began working with her and found out that she had DID stemming from severe abuse in her childhood. She had two primary parts. She was the primary of the day but at night her second primary would come out. His name was Joe and he was a 380 pound African male. When Joe went out he would buy clothing that fit himself and then when he went to bed he would leave the clothing in the closet. It was Joe that was eating in the middle of the night. What she was unaware of was that this other alter was her protector. Her mind had created an alter that's self image that was the most powerful person that she could imagine. By the way Joe was very forthright. I was unable to keep an appointment due to illness. I was bedridden for several days. When the woman arrived for her appointment my secretary simply told her that I was not seeing anyone that week. The second day I was in bed and my wife brought me the phone and on the other end was Joe. He was very upset that I had *blown* off the appointment with Mary. I apologized for not keeping the appointment and asked him to tell Mary how sorry I was and the reason why I was unable to keep the appointment. He was happy and said he would give her the message. Mary was unaware of Joe but Joe was very aware of Mary and he protected her.

There was a middle aged man in front of the mirror. He was three hundred and thirty pounds with short brown hair that was graying. I asked him what he saw as he looked into the mirror. It was comical the way that he viewed himself. He said; "What do you mean? You don't get a body like this without putting a lot of effort into it." When Gary looked into the mirror what he saw was Leo. Leo had long, flowing blond hair and a svelte, highly muscled body. He thought he was a gift to woman; as he put it. He would say it was alright to look, everyone deserved some eye candy. This alter had been created early in his life when he was very athletic. Gary was unable to talk with woman and Leo was created to meet this need. This was a distorted perception of self image. When Gary became Leo he would strut around and act like he was a top model. Leo had not aged in the twenty plus years after being created. Gary had not only aged but had let himself go, tremendously. This is different than the perceptional distorted body image that affects those with conditions like anorexia nervosa. Theirs is initialized by a manic purpose driven need that affects their mind. They are the sole identity of the person. The disassociate has multiple identities, each possessing their own independent perceptional distorted image. The alternate personality's image is created to meet, a survival need of the individual.

The severity of the distortion will be related to the depth of need for the role of the alter. The more predominate the alters role is for the survival of the body and brain of the individual the more ingrained will be the alter self image. Let me give you an example: I had a person come to me that had been severely sexually abused as a child. Her family began molesting her in infancy and by the time she was three years old they had begun using her for bestiality, telling her that she was an animal and not a human. Thirty years later she was so detached from her body that she could not feel any stimulation to her anus or vagina. Her breast and nipples were hyper vigilant against any sensation. The mother of the woman agreed to speak with me and she confirmed that the memories that she was having were in fact accurate. The mother said that while a toddler the father would pinch the Childs breasts to the point of tearing the nipples. The mother had lived in great fear of the abusive man and in an act of self preservation joined with him, helping him in his abuse of the one daughter. The daughter had been used in sex with a variety of animals. In order to cope with this type of abuse the brain created animal alters that would have the sex with the livestock. Because the father would tell her that she was a whore and animal and then reinforce the conditioning by telling her that she liked having sex with the animal, her body would respond to the animals. In order to survive she would have to please her father. He was only pleased by her achieving orgasm with the animals. Because of this human alters were completely detached from the body with complete sensory amnesia. The animal alters were completely hyper sensitive. The father, who practiced hypnotism had used it to put command phrases into the animal alters so that he could say a phrase and snap his fingers and the girl would instantly fugue and the appropriate animal would come out. The father would then use the girl to *put on* shows for paying customers that would come to the farm. These animal alters completely believed they were not human. They did not speak; they only make grunts and sounds appropriate for the animal that they thought they were. These three cases show different aspects of distorted perceptional imagery and how it necessity orientated according to a surviving role function. When a person disassociates the alter will be designed to meet a specific need. The brain will create an image that fits the job requirements.

Another facet of the personal identity is how we are defined by others

A second aspect of personal Identity is the image that we portray to others. It is what we believe others see, when they look at us. Our identity goes beyond just the visual or physical traits that we possess, to include our abilities, limitations, character, class, etc. If an alter needs to have a specific talent in order to fulfill its role it will develop that talent. Because the alter will be performance driven with black and white thinking, it will become the best at that talent. Part of the person's identity is that which we believe others see, if the need to survive is based upon a particular talent, skill or ability the brain will create an alter that will be able to perform that ability. They will be the best at whatever they need to be. It can be music, science, sex, entertainment. The list is endless. This is part of the molding process associated with the personal development of the individual alters. Before going any further I would like to sum up what we have covered thus far.

Dissociation is a survival coping mechanism. When a child prior to the age of seven is placed into a situation of extreme duress or trauma it will cause the life essence to split. Since the personal identity is in the formation stage the split will cause separate identities to be formed. These identities will be molded according to need. The individual self image of the alters will be perceptional distorted to fit the requirements of the role. Each of the alters will be a necessary part of the whole system. The brain will not create an alter that is not necessary. The brain will enable the alters to have skills, talents and abilities to perform their role function to the best of their ability. The alternate personalities will have varying levels of:

a) Conscious awareness –they usually will not be aware of other alters unless their role needs to know about the other alters
b) Intelligence – this is determined by the need capacity
c) Emotion-some are emotionless others overly emotional
d) Mind-some alters can be puppets others have great mind power and facility usage
e) Will some have will power others have none
f) Soul or decision making ability
g) Body sensory attachments

The alter will be purpose, role driven with black and white thinking patterns. They will be a responsive unit with their own personal sets of values and beliefs that will have their own personal definitions and schema.

Alternate personal identities enable a person to fit into society

A person's identity is not always the sum total of how they perceive themselves. It is not uncommon to find in people, who have been deeply wounded, identities that have been split and separated into categories. This divisionary principle allows the person to adapt and fit into a chaotic and separated world. Each of us, are like a puzzle piece. In order to be complete, we need to fit into the greater scheme or picture of the world that we live in. So in essence, identity is not just how we perceive ourselves but also how we express ourselves. It is personal conception with expression. This conception involves both *who we are individually* and also *who we are within a group or affiliation of society*. Our identities are developed as the mind molds and adapts itself, in order to not only survive, but also to thrive. This thriving may even involve acts that are self debasing and de-humanizing. It is a need for acceptance coupled with the need to survive that drives the psyche to create a mind with the ability to do whatever it takes to meet these needs.

On the next page is copy of "Maslow's Hierarchy of Needs."[16] The foundation is the basic needs for physical survival and then with each successive layer another aspect of the personal identity is developed until you get to the top of the structure where the personal values are listed. The personal values will be determined by the lower levels of the pyramid. The need to survive will determine the minds concept and belief in what it means to thrive. Take a moment to study the diagram.

---

[16]Maslow's Hierarchy of Needs: http://en.wikipedia.org/wiki/File:Maslow%27s_Hierarchy_of_Needs.svg

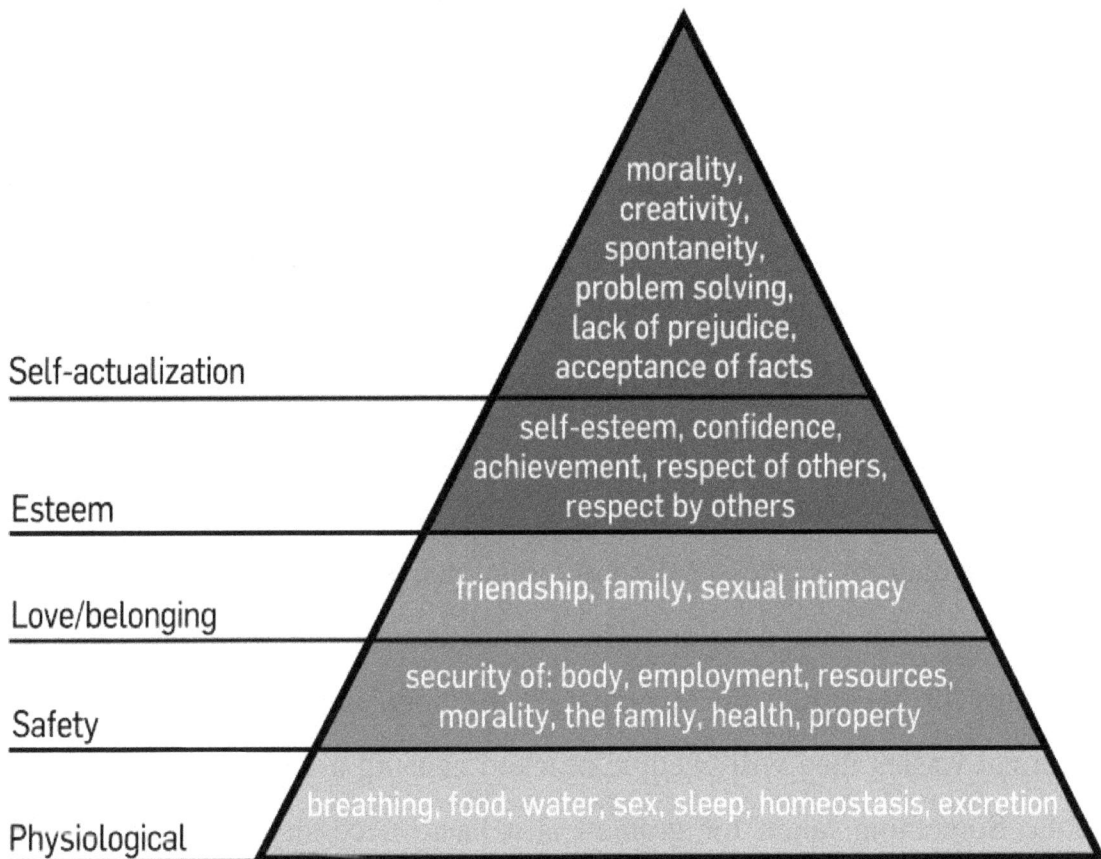

Self-actualization — morality, creativity, spontaneity, problem solving, lack of prejudice, acceptance of facts

Esteem — self-esteem, confidence, achievement, respect of others, respect by others

Love/belonging — friendship, family, sexual intimacy

Safety — security of: body, employment, resources, morality, the family, health, property

Physiological — breathing, food, water, sex, sleep, homeostasis, excretion

➢ The foundation for the structure of needs is physiological. Notice that sex is listed along with homeostasis. Sex is listed as one of the primal needs for survival.

➢ First upon the foundation is the need for safety and to be secure. This need is that which drives the brain to split and dissociate creating an alternative identity to meet the need of the crises ensuring the survival of the whole person.

➤ The second layer upon the foundation is family and friendship along with sexual intimacy. There three will develop in that order.

➤ Everything else will be built upon the first three layers. They will be that which directs and molds the personal identity. In cases of multiple identities the brain will base the formation of the primary splits upon the foundation and secondary splits upon the esteem level.

The above diagram expresses the individual needs of life that must be met in order to survive and develop. The foundation of the pyramid gives the absolutes for basic life. For example, if the body is not allowed to excrete intestinal wastes they will become blocked causing a very slow and painful death. Something taken for granted is a basic necessity for survival. The remaining levels are desired needs, for optimum development of the mind and body. The body can live without employment but the stress of not being actively employed will wear down the will of the individual over time.

If the child is in a home where these needs are met, in a loving, positive, nurturing way, the result will be a dynamic identity that is strong, positive with a good self image. If these needs are not met, the result will be an identity without a strong foundation and an inability to live a life of joy and independence. Many that are deprived of components from the first two tiers never develop the ability for intimacy. They will seem cold, and unaffectionate. They do not possess the ability to give not receive love.

Because they will lack the essential building blocks for a solid foundation the result will be self image that is marred and wounded. This wounded self image will become a perpetual drain of life, hindering the ability to obtain true, continual joy and freedom. The inability to heal these wounds will create within the person a state of helplessness and hopelessness. In the base of the conscious there will be a ball of pain, hatred and rage. This will be the source of upon which value and belief systems of the various alternate identities will be built. It will be a continual source of inner pain, taking a heavy toll upon the person's soul.

The Bible talks about a woman that had been wounded and as a result, her life was in a constant state of being drained. Every day she was dying a little bit more, with no hope or help. She was in a state of helplessness and hopelessness. In a desperate need for healing she had spent her entire life's savings on doctors, but to no avail. It was then that she heard of Jesus the One, Who could heal her. When she learned the truth about Jesus she was given hope to be healed. She was offered that ability to begin living life. It was only when she acted upon this new revelation of truth that she found true healing. By coming to Jesus, the true source of all life that she was healed; the healing came when she touched the Lord.[17] Only Jesus could stop the blood flow and give her the healing she so desperately needed. She had used countless bandages to stop the blood flow but all they ever did was keep her bound. Jesus came and not only healed her but he set her free from the things that bound her. Christ can heal the broken spirit. He can give the

---

[17] Matthew 9:20

person the ability to forgive those that have hurt them, used them and abused them. He can also give them the ability to forgive themselves. He can remove the hatred, pain and bitterness, stopping the continual drain in a person's life. When you come to Jesus and touch Him, then you will be healed, Amen.

The Identity is a combination of both nature and nurture

Another facet of the identity lies in its genesis. The essence of the personal identity is that it is a result, from the combining action of both nature and nurture. *Nature is the genetic and spiritual influence* passed down from the biological parents. This includes generational blessings and also generational curses. *Nurture is what happens* from the point of conception through the adult life. The reason nurture begins at the point of conception is this: Whatever affects the mothers, affects the developing child. The child in the womb is biologically one with the mother. This is a permanent bond that begins physically while the child is in the womb and continues spiritually after the child is born. If the mother experiences fear, pain, trauma, stress, etc., it will directly influence the developing child. This is called neo-natal nurturing. It is what happens in the womb that activates the pre-genetic dispositions. These are called genetic precursors. One example would be the predisposition to disassociate. This is activated in the forming infant while in the womb. Once the predisposition to dissociate is active in a family line; it will be a positive trans-generational trait found in the remaining descendants. This will be a primary trait that will continue to be passed on in the family line, for up to ten generations after the healing has begun. This means it will take ten successive children that have developed the ability to deal with stress without disassociating. In order for this to happen there will have to be no abuse in those ten generations or the cycle will begin again. That is how powerful a genetic precursor is. Because of the centuries of persecution in specific bloodlines they will have primary genetic precursors to instantly disassociate. Those that have this precursor also show potential for hypnosis with high levels of segregated internal thought processes. The predisposition to dissociate is just one of many factoring influences that will compose the development of the psyche foundation. It is from the psyche that the identity will develop. The following are the six components that combine to create the personal identity.

- ☐ The World –its philosophies and systems of beliefs and values
- ☐ The Flesh – a person's own needs and desires
- ☐ The Devil – yes there is a fallen demonic realm that will try to
  Influence, control and if possible destroy a person's life
- ☐ The Family Unit – How the child is treated and raised is the prime
  factor in the personal Identity
- ☐ God and His Word – What a person believes to be true about God,
  their personal concept of God and the belief they have in his
  word, even if they hold the word to be some other book than the
  Bible will greatly affect their personal identity.

☐ Genetic Predispositions [this point may be argued by some] Studies have shown the influence and affect that genetic predispositions play in the development of the personal identity.

Note: Even if a person is not a Christian or born again believer in Christ, it does not mean that their developing mind has not been influenced by the Word of God. In the counseling ministry you will find that many people will have bits of their identity that have been formed from Scriptures and Bible teachings. This holds true even, if they come from areas of the world that are hostile to Christianity or the Holy Bible. For instance, in many countries where Christianity is hated, the prejudice and bias against the Judeo-Christian God and his Holy Bible are foundational building blocks in the no-conscious part of their brain. This is the foundation from which their personal identity is formed. It is common for the Bible to be used in a way contrary to how it was written. Many Bible verses and teachings, when presented to the developing mind of a dissociate have been intentionally misrepresented. They are intentionally misapplied or twisted in order have a negative impact upon the child. This is a common tactic of the devil.

The fallen angelic realm will work to destroy the developing mind

The Devil in an effort to enslave a person will use the Scriptures against them. This is because they are created in God's image. The Devil hates God and he also hates all of mankind, because they bear the image of God. When the Devil uses Christianity to injure a person's developing mind it creates a bitterness and often a hatred for God and the people of God. This is often done by the hand of the abuser. Because there is salvation in no other name than that of Jesus Christ the devil will try to create a hatred for Christ in the child. Also, the instrument that God uses to give us a faith in Christ is by hearing his Holy Word. For this reason the devil will work to create hostility towards the literalness and truth of the Holy Bible.[18] I have heard many times from people that God never helped them when they were being abused or tortured. Because of this they have developed hatred towards God, His word and His people.

NOTE: The devil creates hostility against Christ and the Scriptures in order to enslave the person's mind and emotions because only Jesus Christ can heal and set the person free. It is only by the power of Jesus Christ that their minds can be made whole giving them joy and peace. When God's word is misused the result is pain, bondage and a mind that is separated from God. The foundational belief systems of the person will be formed from a wrong understanding of the true character of God. This leaves the person with an estranged relationship with God the Father, and all too often, a self defeating personality complex."[19]

---

[18] Acts 4:12; Romans 10:17
[19] "Establishing an Identity Founded in Christ," Dr. Tom Knotts; 2011

The brain is a complex, living computer

When trying to understand DID think of the whole picture in terms relating to a computer, since your brain is a living computer. A computer will have many separate programs in it but they all work independently and together contributing to the unit as a whole. Each program will have its own function. The word processor does just that, it is a program designed for processing words. You would not use the financial software for word processing nor would you use a spread sheet, data base system for doing a bible study. You would use the Bible software. Each program has a specific function that makes it unique and important. These programs are designed to carry our specific tasks. In a computer there are always several programs, running simultaneously out of sight of the screen; and so it is with a person that has DID. For instance, a virus program can be running at the same time that a music program is playing. Though they are running concurrent they are doing totally different tasks, with each having its own personal design and function but yet working together as part of the greater whole. The music program is playing music, while the utilities program is scanning for viruses. It is only if the utility find a virus, that they alert the owner to the presence of the virus, and simultaneously quarantining the virus or removing it altogether. Each of the programs work, according to a set of rules; they follow a pre-programmed sequence designed to make the whole unit run smoothly.

The alters within a dissociate are all parts of the greater whole, which together compose the complete person. Though they are split from the main person, they are governed according to a set of rules and confines that are dictated by the internal belief systems within the base of the brain. The chaos that is felt and often demonstrated by the high level dissociate is actually a false representation of what is actually happening. Under all of the chaos, there is an orchestrated set order in how the person's alters work in unison to carry out all of the responsibilities and obligations of the individual whole. To simplify the internal mechanism of the collaborative system the alters are limited to black and white thinking patterns; all of which are based upon logic. The brain works logistically. The alters are extremely focused and task driven. Primary alters will have compulsions driving them to become the best at whatever task they were created for. Like a program designed to run to its ultimate end, primary alters focus on reaching their maximum potential. It is not uncommon to find that once an alter has reached a pinnacle of achievement in their respective field that they will then lose interest in that subject, only to be given a new task by the brain with the whole process starting over again. This is one reason why low level dissociates will have difficulty in keeping the same job for extended periods of time. The brain works to keep the person busy and distracted in order to prevent them from discovering the trauma that is hidden in memory modules in the many different alters. The denial system of the brain has a triggering mechanism that is designed to hide the reality of the person's inner pain. The brain works to keep the person's focus away from the reality of their situation. This is due in part to the established patterns of conflict and denial within each of the alters personal identity. The performance drive is fueled by:

- **Abilities and Inabilities**
- Acceptance and **Rejection**
- Expectations and **Failures**
- **Performance based value and belief systems**

I have personally worked with individuals who have been incredibly gifted and superior in talents and performance than all those around them but they believed that they were simply normal or below standard in their abilities and performance levels. Where a normal person may excel in a single field, and an individual who is gifted may excel in two or three fields but the high end dissociate will rise to the top in a variety of fields. I knew a dissociate who had the following primary alters within his system:

- **Theologian**
- **Psychologist**
- **Demonologist**
- **Preacher**
- **Pastor**
- **Father**
- **Husband**
- **Martial Artist**
- **Musician**

☐ **Cook**

☐ **Thermal Engineer**

☐ **Hard Surface Specialist (flooring specialist)**

☐ **Textual Critic**

☐ **Mechanic**

☐ **Musicologist**

☐ **Writer**

☐ **Editor**

☐ **Researcher**

☐ **And several other fields of work. (He has 48 primary alters in all)**

Dissociation is the brains activating its survival coping mechanism in order to cope with trauma, duress or a situation that otherwise would be unbearable.

There is a positive side to high end dissociation

Not everything about dissociation is negative. There are some qualities that can actually be considered a benefit for the person that is a high end dissociate. For instance a high end dissociate will commonly have an elevated IQ. Their intelligence will be above that of a non-dissociate with a potential continual accelerated learning curve. Because of the ability to dissociate and to create alters that are tailored; to fit the needed role the high end dissociate is almost limitless in the potential. The high level dissociate is able to learn, and master, new information with all the necessary job related skills at an accelerated pace. What may take a non-dissociate several months to learn, the high end dissociate can learn in a few days. They do all of this with a greater depth of expertise than what is possible with a non-dissociate.

The dissociate is a master of adaptation

Another benefit for the high end dissociate is the ability to adapt. The person with DID is like a chameleon, with the potential to adapt and to blend into almost any new situation or circumstance. When placed into an unfamiliar setting, their brain will work to adapt, if necessary the brain will instantly create a new alter for the situation. It will work through the kaleidoscope of information and alters that are situated in the various layers of the brain. It will use a combination of the many different alternate personalities to create a new alter that is *suited* for the occasion.

The kaleidoscope is a term that is used to reference the life force as it flows through a specific combination of alters. If a person has four primary alternate personalities that have been poly-fragmented it will create the potential for a limitless number of alternate personalities that can be created through combining the fragments that are poly-fragmented from the primary alternate personalities. The combined effect of four primary alters gives the brain an incredible amount of knowledge at its disposal. The combining of the poly-fragments is combined with a hyper-analytical sense of logic, coupled with a polished ability for manipulation, so the newly created alter will be able to enter into nearly any conversation or group setting.

When high level dissociate is confronted with a situation that they are unable to deal with, they will appear to be at ease on the outside, but on the inside, their brain and mind's will be working together at an intense pace to create and maintain the new image. Moments like this are very taxing on the person. There are limitations on how long the dissociate can stay in an unplanned situations. Until the new alter is fully developed given its position in the internal scheduling system, their usage will create a great deal of internal stress and conflict. High end dissociates will have an inbuilt schedule, that regulates, when, where, and how they will switch alters. It is a highly regulated system of control that can only be described an ultra micromanagement. The brain and the mind work together to have every detail worked out about what could possibly happen. The brain will equip the alter so that it will be able to handle any of the possibilities of the event. This is part of the preparation for the role. The brain does not like surprises and in highly regulated system, any surprises will already be pre-programmed into the scripts that are prepared for the new alter. Because of the brains need to be in control of everything, it will maintain a rigid schedule. Even the times of flexibility in the schedule will have been prepared and then placed into a pre-approved time slot. This is the reason that a high end dissociate will struggle with the amount of time that they can hold themselves together when placed into an unfamiliar situation or circumstance they are not prepared for. It takes a great deal of mental energy to maintain a high end system, especially if that system has internal alters that are simultaneously working on complex projects in the unconscious part of the brain leaving the presenting alter to deal with the new or uncertain situations. The dissociates systems work best when everything runs according to a schedule. The alters function best in their appointed time slot.

A high end dissociate needs time to defragment and reboot his systems

One negative aspect of being a dissociate is that when the dissociates systems becomes overly stressed or challenged, they will lose their ability to interact with others for extended periods of time. Having to maintain the vigil, of a normal appearance takes a heavy toll on the inner workings of the mind with the varying states of consciousness. The mind will grow weary. In order to rectify the wear on the systems, there will be a preprogrammed mechanism within the structure of the no-conscious. This system of maintenance will consist of utilities that will work in developing and molding the many alters. When memories need to be separated and stored, the no-conscious part of the brain will cause the person to separate and withdraw from others for what is referred to as, *down time.* It is while in this down time that memories will either be allocated to the proper alter and then placed into long term storage or they will be destroyed and flushed out of the memory system. Any scripts that need to be put in place or new scripts that need to be written will be handled during the down time.

NOTE: The high end dissociate will need to have regular periods of time where they separate from everyone else, drawing into their own world. This time of separation can take many forms. For some it can be listening to music, watching television, or some other form of mental catharsis where they shut down and simply take in the self-prescribed form of stimulus relief. For other dissociates it can be in the form of doing something physical like dance, martial arts, gardening, long bike rides or even extreme sports where they are given a high doses of adrenaline. During this period of down time the brain will go through all the information that has been gathered and begins a serious of informational and statistical analysis and filtering. Like a computer that has been programmed to continually learn from its environment the dissociate brain will take all of the new information with the perceptional stimulus and will then analyze it before, processing and acclimating it to the proper alters. It will then implement the new information into its presenting strategies. All information that is unnecessary or dangerous to the integrity of the systems will be destroyed and flushed from the mind and memory. I have known of dissociates that would do extreme sports for their cathartic withdrawal. The down time can take on any form of personal entertainment or recreation that allows the inner conscious, in collaboration with the brain, to withdraw and reorganize the internal systems.

The disassociates life is a facade

The life of a dissociate will appear to be very structured, some would even call it module. They will exemplify how a person should act and live, but this is not the true person that you are seeing. This is a front that has been prepared. When the internal systems begin to become worn, over stressed or challenged they will begin to exhibit signs of depression, hyper-criticalness, bitterness, anger, negativity and all of the other works of the flesh.[20] In low level dissociation it is common to show traits, or to exhibit bi-polar.[21] Extreme mood swings with bouts of continual, emotional upheavals and outbursts are a normal part, of many dissociate lives. Often, they will have several other disorders, such as addictions, phobias, and compulsions that will come and go routinely. Each alter will have its own state of conscious and its own particular way of dealing with stress. They will each have their own personal compulsions or addictions. It is common in counseling to have, extremely depressed alters and ecstatically happy alters, within the same person, that will switch back and forth during a counseling session. It is this characteristic that causes the person to be misdiagnosed as bi-polar instead of having DID. When the client goes from extreme depression to euphoria in the same session it gives all the appearance to the counselor that they are suffering from a chemical imbalance. This in turn motivates the counselor to refer the client for a medication based treatment.

After a high level dissociate is placed on the medications they find little relief from their problems. I have heard many dissociates say that they still have the problems, but the *drugs* make them feel better, or not feel at all. Since it is the only option they have for relief it becomes the primary method use to deal with the hidden internal conflicts. Medicating someone does not fix the problem it only helps the person to ignore it. True healing

---

[20] Galatians 5:19-ff.
[21] Note: Once the person has been brought to healing and integration the bi-polar is healed

comes from identifying the problem and then Scripturally offering them the solution. I spoke with a well recognized psychiatrist on this subject. She was wanting to keep a high level dissociate on medications for *"their own good."* The person was so over medicated they could not function. When I told the psychiatrist that the client was a high level dissociate with several hundred personalities she informed me that; "Dissociation was a myth. It was so rare to find someone with DID that is really did not exist." She was wrong and after getting the man off the six different prescriptions he was, not only able to function, but he obtained employment and through therapy we were able to work through many of the reasons for the initial splits in his consciousness, bringing his alters to healing and integration. When I confronted the psychiatrist about the client having DID she lost her composure and even threatened to send the law to have me arrested if I interfered in her treatment with her client, who she said was unable to make decisions for himself. She stated that if he did not take the medications that her next step would be to refer him for residency in the state mental facility. I did interfere with her client and as a result the man is happy, working and off the medications; by the way he sleeps well every night now without medication. This man had been misdiagnosed. When he had originally went to see the psychiatrist his chief complaint was that his brain would not shut down so that he could sleep. He had actually been awake for over two weeks straight with little down time! She diagnosed him as being a paranoid schizophrenic labeling him as a danger to himself and others. Her diagnosis was not only wrong but if I had not of seen him and properly diagnosed the man, he could have ended up being permanently confined to a mental facility.

Medications can and often do help initially. For instance the man discussed above did need to have his brain shut down in order to be able to work with him. The medications did this. The first day he was given the medications he slept for over 17 hours before waking up for two hours and then falling back to sleep for another 14 hours. He was very heavily medicated. His brain needed to be shut down for a period of rest; but he did not need to be placed onto medication for the rest of his life. What he needed was healing and integration.

When working with a dissociate each alter must be dealt with personally. The key to helping them is to find what it was that caused the original split of the psyche. The initial trauma will be the wedge that has been driven into the no-conscious part of the brain separating the life essence, creating two separate identities. By releasing the traumatic stress that has caused the wedge the problem will be alleviated allowing for healing and integration to occur.

NOTE: The trauma that causes the initial split is like a wedge driving into the conscious that separates the life essence creating two areas of conscious. The main conscious will be shut down and placed into a state of fugue while the newly created conscious will become and alternate identity that will be molded to deal with the traumatic event. It will be designed to deal with that trauma, and any future trauma of that particular nature that re-occurs.

There are many different types of alters that can be created through dissociation but there are only six different types of dissociation.

☐ Dissociative Amnesia

☐ Dissociative Fugue

☐ Dissociative Identity Disorder

☐ Depersonalization Disorder

☐ Dissociative Trance Disorder

☐ Dissociate Disorder Not Otherwise Specified

Prepare yourself to help your client

Dissociation can occur from a single act of conflict or trauma to the psyche. This is often the case with those who are a simple dissociate that has experienced fragmentation. The complex dissociate is the progeny of many instances of trauma, neglect or abuse. The brain will resort to all six types of dissociation as a means of coping with repetitive occurrences of abuse or trauma. Here is a problem area in counseling. Because of a lack of experience and/or training with dissociation, counselors have a great deal of difficulty in identifying and treating the specific type of dissociation that their client has experienced. When a client presents several different alters, each with their own list of particular varying symptoms, it can become confusing and hard to identify the type of dissociation that has occurred. This is because the client has actually undergone several different types of dissociation, working together to achieve the desired results.

Here is an illustration: The dissociate may have one alter, named bill that has amnesia but then also they have a different alter named sue that is showing all the characteristics of suppression. These are two different types of dissociation and they stem from two very different coping mechanism needs for survival. The person may also have a third, primary alter named Ted that is completely detached from his body and emotions, which is another dissociative condition. In order to treat the client you will have to work with Bill, Sue and Ted all differently. This is why the counselor needs a solid grasp of the dissociative states. Another important element for the counselor is a good understanding of the terminology associated with dissociative conditions. Counselors should all be familiar with the following terms:

☐ Amnesia
☐ Suppression
☐ Repression
☐ Depersonalization
☐ Detachment
☐ Dissociation
☐ Fugue

By the counselor having a thorough understanding of the various types of dissociation, they will better understand the root of the dissociative states. It's important to remember that no two cases are the same. There may, and will be similarities between cases but that is all it is; a similarities. Each case is unique, just as each person is unique.

When you approach the work of identifying the dissociative condition take into consideration the fact that, the Dissociative Disorder ***is a disruption*** in the usually integrated functions of consciousness, memory, identity, of the perceptions of the environment that the individual is in. A common trait of the disorder is that the person will hear voices in their heads telling them what they should or should not do. This is not schizophrenia. In schizophrenia the voices are outside of the head, and attached to, or allocated to, specific items, spirits and/or demons. In DID the voices are located inside the persons head similar to an overly active and loud sub-conscious. The voices are not the sub-conscious but are actually the various alters, voicing their opinions and thoughts. This causes a great deal of chaos and disturbance for the individual. They often will say such things as, "I feel like I'm going crazy" *or* "I can't get the voices out of my head!" These disturbances may happen suddenly to where the person just begins hearing them all at once or they may come on slowly with a gradual heightening in intensity. This is the nature of the disorder. It is a separation of the conscious functions of the person, from a single camerality to a bi-cameral, tri-cameral or quadrin-camerality. This separation point happens below the fifth layer of the conscious which is located between the no-conscious and the un-conscious parts of the brain. The next chapter is devoted to the identifying characteristics of each of the various types of dissociation, beginning with Dissociative Amnesia.

Chapter Three: The Six Types of Dissociation

"I've never been able to remember that year of my life. For some reason, I can remember my childhood in great detail but I keep thinking something must have happened to me when I was twelve years old, what it is, I just don't know." This young lady had came to me with an OCD[22] that I believed was stemming from her childhood, so I began to ask her questions about her early years. She was very bright and intelligent, possessing an incredibly detailed memory. She was able to give me a detailed account of her early years of life and also about her later teen years but for some reason, when she got to her eleventh and twelfth years of age she would go blank. Her facial expression became blank, her face palled and she responded in a somewhat monotone voice that she did not have any memories of those years. The questions I asked her were triggering a defense and denial system within her brain. Something irrecoverable had happened to her memories during that period of time in her life. I believed that the key to her OCD was locked away in those memories. Something had happened to her, in that short period of time that had changed her life. It was in her thirteenth year that thoughts began emerging in her mind that contradicted all of her Christian beliefs. These thoughts were coupled with urges that were also contrary to what she knew to be appropriate and acceptable behavior. These thoughts began evolving from ideations into an erratic OCD. I began to

---

[22] Obsessive Compulsive Disorder

explore those missing years of memory and as I did I noticed that her body image shifted. Her for-head tightened and one eye closing down a bit. These are facial expressions of inner turmoil with a repression of memory. We prayed and asked the Lord to reveal, what it was, that was the root of her problem; the visual memories all began to come back. The pictures and body memories began coming into her conscious, a little at first but then they broke loose and began flooding her mind. She was overcome with emotion and folded over in tears, holding her arms around herself tightly like a small child.

What had happened to this young lady was that when she was 12 years old, her parents had sent her to a Christian Camp for the summer. During her time at camp the female counselor that was assigned to her began molesting her. This happened, not once but over and over, every night and sometimes during the day also. This continued the entire summer in the *Christian Camp*. As she began telling me about what had happened to her, she remembered that in her later teen years she would have this reoccurring nightmare that someone was laying on top of her, kissing her all the way down her body until they reached her genital area where they would then begin performing oral sex on her. She remembered that she would wake from these nightmares, feeling very sexually aroused but also incredibly ashamed. This young lady had been brought up in the Christian faith where it was taught that a person was to remain a virgin until marriage saving themselves for their one true love. She was very devoted to her Christian beliefs. The problem was, that this camp counselor was someone that she had trusted and admired. Around the camp the counselor would act very religious, quoting the Scriptures and correcting the teens, helping them with their problems and appearing to everyone to be this wonderful loving person. But whenever she got this young lady alone she would immediately begin molesting her. What the young lady did not know, is that she was already a dissociate, before going to the camp and that she had several alters already within her that had been sexually abused. The conflict and denial within her mind was between her two alters. The alternate personalities that did not know this counselor was a pedophile, respected her as a good Christian and someone that they could put their trust in, but to the alters that were being molested she was a sick and twisted individual that abused children. This young woman came from a family whose culture accepted and practiced incest. It was not until she was twelve years old that her family had accepted Christ as their Savior and embraced the Christian way of life. Because of the former molestation from the hands of the father, mother and brother, who had all sexually abused her, she had several primary alternate personalities. To complicated the matter, some of her alters were very sexual, looking forward to the encounters with the counselor and even initiating some of them. The culture she was raised in, was one in which the young girls were considered to be property of the father who would train them in sexual practice. The woman were to be trained as servants for the men to be used sexually, whenever and however, the men over them desired. Though her family had converted to Christianity, they were still practicing their cultural beliefs about woman and sexuality.

When the molestation happened, it created, not only confusion within her mind by going against her religious beliefs, but it created an incredible conflict, because, though she knew that it was wrong, her body would respond to the sexual acts, often having several orgasms with each encounter.[23] It was after, she had alters that came to salvation in Christ Jesus that the true conflict began in her sub-conscious, as some alters where created and trained to be used sexually but alters that were created to fulfill the Christian role were pure in heart with a focus of living for Jesus Christ. The mind could not take the incredible conflict when these two very separate worlds collided. Here was someone that should have been trusted as a Christian counselor but instead of acting righteous they were actively using her like an abuser. The knowledge of this would have destroyed the Christian alters ability to perform their role as devoted children of God so the brain protected them by keeping the Christian parts ignorant of what was happening to her body. This was done through dissociative amnesia.

The dissociate amnesia began, because a part of her knew that the molestation was wrong, and that it should not have been happening to her, from the hands of a trusted Christian counselor. But inside of her was another alter that would become extremely aroused by the abuse, giving itself over to the abuser and having multiple orgasms as a result. This internal conflict began overwhelming her with feelings of guilt and shame. Though she knew it was wrong, she could not stop her body from enjoying the sexual experiences. To compound the issues, the one who should be

---

[23] She had been trained and conditioned by her father to have strong sexual desires and multiple climaxes

leading her in paths of righteousness and obedience to the Lord was the very one raping her. This created all the elements for the brain to dissociate the mind and memories. The OCD began after she left camp. During her month long stay at the Christian camp, her body and brain had become conditioned from the repetitive acts of abuse so that they desired the sexual experiences. The act of orgasmic release can be very addicting to the brain.

When a person undergoes ritual abuse,[24] that is sexual in nature several things happen within the brain that will contribute to the dissociative amnesia. The first is the link between the pain and pleasure centers in the brain. There is a link between the pain and pleasure centers of the brain in the rewards center. The limbic system of the brain controls:

1) The Endocrine system
2) The Autonomic Nervous System
3) The Nucleus Accumbens
4) The Brain Pleasure Center

The Limbic system is composed of:
1) The Hippocampus
2) The Amygdale
3) The Fortex
4) The Septal Nuclei

[24] Ritual Abuse is abuse that happens in accordance with social custom or as normal protocol, i.e. it happens repeatedly

5) The Mammilliary Body

6) The Limbic Lobe

7) The Para hippocampus Gyrus

8) The Cingulate Gyrus

9) The Dentate Gyrus

10)   The Entorhinal Cortex

11)   The Piriform Cortex

12)   The Fornicate Gyrus

13)   The Orbital Frontal Cortex

14)   The Limbic is also interconnected with the prefrontal Cortex

When a person undergoes trauma it affects the entire body. The brain is the processing unit that allocates and directs the entire stimulus that the person experiences. These affected areas are:

1) Physical-pain, pleasure numbness and the ability to detach from all physical sensation. In some cases sensory amnesia can result to the afflicted area/s.

2) Spiritual-the spirit of the person can become broken to the point that they feel helpless, hopeless and completely overwhelmed by their situation. When this happens the mind becomes detached from the body and spirit and dissociates the trauma and experience from the person. This is the apex *of depersonalization*, where the spirit must be given the ability to live or it will give up and die. A crushed spirit can

cause the autonomic systems to shut down and the person will simply curl up and die. This was documented by those during World War II that were subjected to extreme deprivation, and or durational trauma. Once their spirit was crushed they lost the will to live and the bodies systems shut down and they died.

3) Emotional- when the emotions become very intensely affected it causes deep fissure scarring. This is the result of very intense memories. These memories are visual, emotional, and physical. To protect the mind of the victim, the brain instantly separates the memories, creating a dissociative neural pathway for these new memories to travel alone with a newly created storage point, which is called the modeling center. This self defense mechanism works in conjunction with the coping mechanism to ensure the protection of the person's mind. If the mind is not separated and then shielded from these traumatic experiences, the result would be a complete shattering of the spirit; i.e. the will to live would be lost, causing the autonomic systems to cease. The body would shut down and the person would die. In experiments conducted by the late Joseph Mengale, on the splitting of the conscious, it was found that there was a threshold barrier point, that when crossed would result in the shattering of the spirit, causing the victim to curl up in a fetal position and to die. Their minds and bodies shut down because their spirit lost the will to live. Schizophrenic catatonic states are the result of the brain activating a last line of defense to ensure the survival of the person. In order to

live the brain orders a complete detachment and shutting down of all ability to give or receive perception and or stimulus. The mind is pulled inside and completely severed and shielded from all outside influence. The mind is then placed into a world that is created by the no-conscious part of the brain, placing the person in a semi-hibernation state. This is a complete, mind, body and spirit detachment.

The utilities for a dissociate are the systems that are in place

When a person is a high level dissociate there will be several systems that control the function of the cooperate body as a whole. A system is a group of non-cognoscente functions, that work together to reach a desired result. Each primary alter will have its own systems. The system in place for a primary will also be over all of the other splits that come out of them. Other splits would include secondary, trilinary and quadrinary alters and all mental and body fragment memories; as in the case of poly-fragmentation. The systems work towards maintaining a state of, optimum level of harmonious congruency within the alters system and homeostasis for the body. This is achieved by keeping a strict regimen with routine procedures that are designed to trigger when something unexpected happens. The following are the various components of systems that can be found within the dissociate. The complexity of the internal framwork will determine how many facets the system will have.

➢ Denial -The denial system works to keep the individual ignorant and oblivious to what is happening to them physically, emotionally, spiritually and mentally. Denial also keeps the other alters from being able to detect or become aware of each other along with their function and purpose for existence. A person's denial system can keep them from knowing something is happening even when it is right in front of them. I was called by a woman that was a dissociate and asked to come and talk with her abuser to calm him down. He had a habit of being angry when he got home and she was particularily afraid this night. I had only had two sessions with her at the church and had not gotten to the root of her problem. I did not know she was being abused by this man as she had never told me. When I asked if he was abusing her she said no, he just yells a lot. When I got to the home I could hear him screaming at her and her pleading with him. I went straight into the home and found that he had her pinned with her arm twisted behind her back and up to her head. He was trying to break her arm and just as I came through the door he punched her in the head. I came straight at him and told him to turn her loose. He jumped up and threatened me. I stepped between her an him and told him if he wanted to attack me to do it because I would put him down. (I know it does not sound to professional at this point, but working in the prison system taught me one thing, you have to stand your ground or you will get hurt). He went out of the house telling me he was going to slash all of my tires. I lifted the woman up and sat her down. She had been beaten quite severally. I told her that we needed to call the police and make a report. I told her that she could not allow him to abuse her like this. As I was speaking she switched alters as her eyes glazed over and she sat up and said, "_____ does not abuse me, he loves me. He just get angry and yells a lot." I told her that she that he almost broke her arm and that her mouth was bleeding to just look into the mirror. (She had one on the wall next to the table). She looks into the mirror and responds, "Pastor I don't know what's wrong with you but you should not falsely accuse _____. There's nothing wrong with me and like I said he has never laid a hand on me." She asked me to leave her home because she was upset I came in without being invited. I waited outside and called the police. The arriving officers confirmed the severity of her abuse and issued a warrant for the man. She was in a state of denial. She could look at the evidence, of the blood running out of her mouth and a bald spot where he had ripped her hair out, but when she looked in the mirror she saw no blood, bruises or a bald spot. Because she found her security and in this man and her identity had been formed from an abusive life, she had a denial system in place that kept her ignorant of her circumstance. To her mind it was better to be with the man, who loved her, than it would be to be on her own and alone. Children that have been abused in the formative stages of growth will often have a mind reversal. Pain will replace pleasure, hatred will replace love and so on. This negative foundation is a part of a denial system. It arises from the first two layers of Maslow's hierarchy of needs.

➢ Scripts- Scripts are stories and alibis that are designed for the purpose of explaining lost time during fugue episodes. They fill in the blank for the presenting alter when it is placed in fugue so another primary or secondary alter can do its job. For instance, I worked with a female who was a slave. She was used in sex trafficking by her owner. Her father had raped and molested her all of her life, beginning in infancy and had made a living off of selling her to others. When she was still a teenager she was on the accepted list to several night clubs. These were the clubs were people would stand outside all night hoping to get in. She was on the list so that she could just drive up and a person would park her car and she would be ushered in. She was not allowed to drink so this was never a issue. She would go into the clubs and would then be used by groups of men for sex in the back and upper rooms of these establishments. The primary presenting alter was completely unaware of this. She thought that she was just going into these clubs and dancing the night away. She even bragged on the fact that her father never complained about her going or how late she stayed out. While the sexual slave alter was doing her job in the back and upper rooms of the night clubs the script in her head told her that she was dancing the night away. This script also explained why her body would be bruised and sore the next few days. A good example of a running script is in the form of a stage show hypnotist. A hypnotist can talk with the no-conscious part of a person brain making it believe it is a chicken, monkey or anything. While on stage clucking away the person goes into a fugue state where they do not even know that their bodies are waddling around the stage like a duck. They think they have been sitting the whole time waiting for the hypnotist to do something. Scripts provides stories that the mind of the alter will believe happened rather than letting them face the truth. This prevents unnecessary stress and unwanted concerns to the brain and psyche. The brains number one concern is to keep the person alive and healthy. That is why it produces scripts. The script allows the alters to do their job while maintaining their anonymity. Scripts work together with denial making a single system.

➢ Fugue- Fugue is when the active conscious of the presenting alter of a dissociate goes into a state of semi-hibernation. During this time period is will be pulled back into the fourth layer of the unconscious part of the brain where it will be separated from all perceptional influence for the duration of the fugue. During fugue, all time will be stopped; the alter will be oblivious to everything that is happening during the duration of the state of fugue. None of the memories will in any way be allocated or given association with the alter that is in the state of fugue. The alter that is in the state of fugue will be replaced with another alternate identity that will act as, representation for the body. The proper alter will be in control of the active conscious performing its role. All memories will be allocated and associated to the active alternate personality with segregation boundaries placed around them until they can be put into their holding memory modules. Any actions or memories that can cause further fragmenting of the alter will be discarded and flushed from the system,

> Guardian -The guardian an alter that is created to protect and guard the structure of the individual alters. In high level dissociation an alter can be created by the mind for this purpose. In mind control programming there will be several guardians put in place by the programmer. Their role will be to prevent the discovering of any programming in the individuals mind. Some of the ways they divert attention is by creating a histrionic response with the individual. They will wear their emotions on their sleeve, over reacting when a person gets close to discovering any of the inner secrets. In some individuals there will be a box or housing unit, at the very bottom of the no-conscious layer of the brain, just above the brain stem. The Guardian will often be a dark covering over this box, keeping it hidden from discovery. Inside the box or holding unit will be all the memories, both mental and physical memories. This is why any releasing can cause a re-experiencing of painful body memories coupled with all the emotions the person endured during the trauma. This box will contain all of the hatred, pain, anguish, rage and bitterness. Everything that was too painful for the alter to endure will be in this box. The body and mind will have been detached from everything in this box. When this box or unit is opened the person may experience flooding.

Flooding is when everything they have separated from and hidden away comes flooding back into their mind and they relive it all over again. All of it in one big burst. Often this is too much for the person's mind and body to endure and they shut down. This is why the psyche creates a Guardian to keep the holding unit hidden. The original paint hat caused the first dissociative split will be held in this box. It will be the seat of the shattered and torn heart. To have final healing it must be dealt with. The impact can be lessened by working through the alters and their worlds from the top down to the box. In this way the load is lifted from the box a little at a time so that when you get to the bottom you only have to deal with the primeval splits. from will be under the watch of the guardian. There is also another kind of Guardian that is created and designed to watch over and protect the mind, will, emotions and body of the person, as a whole. I have seen guardians come out in individuals before. I saw a very thin woman in the first church I was in, who loved an elderly lady very much come to her defense. I did not know it but there was a man who was very rude to this elderly woman and one day I heard a commotion, as I got into the entry way the thin woman had this 200 plus pound man lifted into the air by one arm, telling him loudly, "You will not hurt grandma!" With one hand she lifted him off the ground and slammed him into the wall. She was a high level dissociate with a Guardian in her that would not allow anyone to hurt the person she loved.

- The librarian-the librarian is the alter that houses all of the information and knowledge of the various alters within the person. When an alter is performing its role or doing a job the librarian will upload the information that it needs in order to fulfill its role. It is the librarian that will also do research for the alters. The librarian does not always have human form. Many times it will simply look like a door, that when opened is a series of book shelves, computers or other forms of storage.

- The Switcher-the Switcher is an alter that controls the triggering of the alters and also cues alters when they are to go up to the active conscious or that retracts them back into the lower layer of the unconscious. The switcher plays a very important part in managing the alters. In high level dissociation the switcher can create any number of combinations of alters by combining alters. According to Boole's theory of analytical mathematics an infinite number of alters can be created from combining four pyramids. In high level disassociation where there is mind control programming, it is common for there to be four primary alters with four secondary alters split from each of them and a additional three trilinary alters split from each of the four secondary splits and then twelve splits from each of the three trilinary alters. The mixture only involves the four sets of quadrinary alters. They are tied together through the three trilinary alters from each of the four secondary alters. When the life energy is directed by the center control mechanism it can combine the *kalidescope* of alters into an infinite number of possible combinations. These combinations will have a precise application of mind, will, emotion, intellect and bodily skill. This is the fabric from which the chameleon ability rises.

- ➤ The internal clock mechanism-This is a regulation mechanism that controls when alters are asleep or awake. For instance the main presenting alter can be in a deep sleep but the internal clock mechanism can be set to completely wake up the body at 3 am for the proper alter to control the body to perform its role. I have worked with many high level dissociates that had internal clock mechanisms. They would be unaware that they were doing satanic rituals in the middle of the night, such as being used for sodomy, the eating of feces and drinking of urine. This internal clock mechanism works with all of the previously mentioned components.

- ➤ The keeper of the secrets-In disassociates that have been ritually abused there will usually be one alter that has knowledge of everything. This alter will live according to the rules; speak no evil, see no evil, hear no evil. Many times it will not have a face or will be missing the eyes, ears and mouth. The reason for this is that the person's survival is often tied to their ability to keep secrets; especially in cults or secret organizations. Since the brain needs to remember those things that are pertinent to its survival the keeper of the secret will be the alter that holds all of the information. In mind control programming the alter will be conditioned to never reveal anything to any person that does not have direct authority from their owner. The reinforcement conditioning is usually in the form of extreme torturous imposed methods. I have known a man that was nearly drowned several times and then completely drowned five times. They would bring him back to life and give him a short period in which they would reinforce their directives then they would physically drown him to make it a permanent part of his internal programming. This is just one method that is used.

➢ The Brain-The brain will often view itself as being something other than what it is. In the early years of life, those prior to 3 or 4 years of age, the child that is severally abused can so completely detach itself that the brain will hide itself in another form. I have found brains that viewed themselves as cartoon characters, robots, beasts and many other forms. The brain does this so that it can control the various alters with no remorse or guilt. For instance, if the person is being used for bestiality the brain, because it believes it is a robot or some other thing or character, will have problem sending a child alter into a pig pen to be used sexually by the animal. The brain is completely detached and does not even view itself as a part of the person. In mind control programming it is common for programmers to clone themselves into the brain so that the brain will keep the person in slavery, doing everything the programmer has conditioned them to do, even long after the programmer has died. I have worked with high level dissociates that were programmed in the early fifties and sixties that still had the clone of their programmer inside of them, commanding them and keeping everything running smoothly.

➤ The Heart-It is not uncommon to find the heart of a dissociate to be connected to only one or a select few alters. The heart is listed as a separate component because it is the seat of emotions. In detachment disorders there will be degrees of feeling and emotions that are allocated to each of the individual alters. The alters in control of the heart will typically be the first four primary splits. These four alters will be the oldest of the alters in the person for this reason they will be buried in the deepest layers of the subconscious. In RA[25], or SRA-DID the heart will be layered like an artichoke with each layer being a complete point of separation created through trauma so severe that the alter dies and another is split out of it forming another layer. The heart is not allowed to stop. High level mind control programming will use technology to train the heart to respond to commands, gestures or other non-verbal means to slow down, shut down, or speed up. The heart control programming is done through the alters that are tied to the heart. The autonomic systems are programmed using neural linguistic programming methods.

➤ The worlds-Worlds are created as homes and safe places where the primary alters dwell surrounded by all of their poly-fragmented splits. It is the place where the alter will escape from reality, drawing into a fantasy world while an alter that is split from it goes to be the

---

[25] Ritual abuse

presenting alter to perform its role. It is kept separated from the trauma and abuse by staying in its individual world while the quadrinary splits merge with those surrounding other worlds to create alters that can do the best job possible.

All of these systems work together to keep harmony in the mind of the dissociate. They cannot be separated in function without affecting all of the other systems in the brain and body.

The roots of dissociate amnesia run deep

When a child is dissociated through ritual abuse the brain will use dissociative amnesia to protect the young child's mind, this is especially true is the abuser is a member of the child's immediate family. A young child's[26] limbic system is not equipped to handle sexual stimulation; it is not developed for sexual stimulation. When this occurs, the brain dissociates the trauma from the child's active conscious and creates an alternate identity to deal with the abuse. This new alter will be identified with the abuse. By separating the child from the abuse through dissociation they are not in any way associated with the abuse, so they are safe and unharmed, even though it is their body that is being abused they are unaware of it. Since it is happening to the new alternate personality they know nothing about it. This initial split has now created two separate primary identities. The first being the child's active conscious prior to the abuse. The child will be dissociated

---

[26] A child prior to the age of eight years of age, circa.

80

and placed into a world where it will exist in a state of fugue until the trauma is over. The mind of the child will have the memories of the initial trauma, that caused the dissociation severed from them through amnesia. The new alternate personality will be the second primary alter. It will have its own world created to house it after the trauma is over. Everything that happens during the traumatic period will be allocated and assigned to this new trauma. Its identity will be created and molded by this experience. If it is used for being beaten, than that's what its role will be. It will believe its reason for existing is to be beaten. It will find its value through this. When the abuse is over the new alter will go down to its newly created world and when it goes down the original alter will piston up back into the conscious, coming out of fugue, oblivious to anything that has transpired.

The mechanisms will begin to be connected to the internal alters

Alters that are not in use will be drawn into their own world. The only time the alternate personalities leave their worlds and rise to the surface of the conscious is when they are triggered to do so.

NOTE: In cases of simple dissociation there will not be worlds created. Simple dissociation is when there is only one primary alter and less than four secondary alters. In this case the secondary alters will stay in the third and fourth layer of the mind. These are called the anterior of the sub-conscious, (the third layer) and the un-conscious, (the fourth layer) of the mind. The person will hear voices inside of their head when the secondary alters rise to the sub-conscious, (the second layer) of the mind. When this happens the secondary alters are putting in their input, voicing their concerns and opinions to the primary alter. A complex dissociate is different than a simple dissociate in this one point; the complex will be created through ritual abuse. They will have more than one primary identity. The complex will have an internal housing system for each of the primary identities. These housing units can look like any type of residence, world, country, or place that can be inhabited.   [Now back to the mechanics of triggering]

When a young child endures ritual abuse it will become poly-fragmented. This poly-fragmenting makes the child into a complex dissociate. A complex dissociate will have worlds in which the fragmented parts all dwell in around the primary alter. These alters will have a triggering effect that is attached to them, which will pull them to the surface when they are needed to perform their role. Here is an example of a triggering mechanism.

When a child is routinely molested by an individual at night the mind identifies the pattern of abuse and assigns triggers from the pattern of abuse to the proper individual identities so they can better perform their role. By allocating function and roles to specific alter the brain creates a secure environment. By keeping all the same groupings of splits from the same primary identity and housing them all in the same world the brain and mind can function at a higher rate of speed. This is essential in keeping the alters separated and protecting their anonymity. I had a client that father would molest them every night after their mother would leave for work. Her mother would leave at 9 pm for work and after her mother left her father would come to her room to molest her.

Her first trigger: the mother leaving for work

When she would hear her mother leave she would go into a fugue state: This was her first trigger; her mother leaving the home triggered her mind to get ready for the abuse.

This would bring up the secondary alter called *"Daddy's Girl,"*. Her father would begin walking up the stairs and daddy's girl would hear him, this would trigger the secondary alter to be brought up to the surface with daddy's girl going back down. This alter would deal with the fear of the father coming upstairs. The father would enter the room and depending on what he would do, the effect would be the appropriate alter would rise to the surface.

If he wanted to beat her, than an alter that was physically detached would come to the surface.

If he wanted oral sex than an alter would come to the surface that thought his penis was a orange popsicle would come to the surface. It loved to lick the popsicle. This was important because if she did not put her whole heart into it, showing that she was, as he put it , "a whore," then he would have to beat her and punish her for being a bad girl. This girl would not choke when he put his penis all the way down her throat.

If he wanted to hurt her with a pencil or other object than she had another part that would come up that could not feel pain. It would hold itself so that he could hurt the body. This part had a sister that would come out after everything was over to take the bedding downstairs, where she would wash it. It was her job to clean up everything so the mommy would not find any blood or suspect anything.

After putting the sheets back on the bed the child would go to sleep and go to sleep. When she awoke in the morning she would remember nothing, because she had nothing to remember. It had never happened to her. The alternate identities were the ones that had been used and abused. They were the ones with the pain and memories.

Once again a child that is ritually abused will have specific triggering mechanisms attached to the individual alters. A trigger can be when the child hears the persons footsteps coming to their room at night the alter that has been created for the abuse will rise to the active conscious, the main person is placed into a fugue state, and the alter that has been created for the trauma will perform its role during the abuse. When it is a reoccurring pattern it is classified as ritual abuse even when it is considered normal in the person cultural society. The family may be at ease, in an incestuous relationship but the brain of the child is still unequipped to deal with sexual stimulation and the result is injury to the brain, a separating of the conscious and the creating of an alternate identity for interfacing with the abuser and storing all of the memories of the incidents.

How a slave is made

When a woman is sexually stimulated the periaqueductal gray area of the brain stem is activated. This is the area of the brain that controls the fight or flight response. This is because a woman's brain needs to know that it is safe and is going to be protected when it is being sexually stimulated. When a woman has an orgasm the area behind their left eye, called the lateral orbital frontal cortex completely shuts down taking away their ability to make decisions. This is the area of the brain that is called the seat of decisions. When the lateral orbital frontal cortex shuts down they lose their abilities to make decisions. This area, is the brains seat of reason and also the area that houses, the behavioral control center. A young child that is dissociated and sexually stimulated will lose their ability to control their behavior and to make decisions. Their body will respond to the physical sexual stimulation. The periaqueductal gray area will activate the fight or flight response causing dissociative identity disorder and the alter that is created, will not have the ability to make its own decisions nor to control their behavior, this is why it is by the purity of the definition; a form of programming when the child goes through ritual abuse. The alter that is created will completely be given over to the will of their abuser. They will become whatever their abuser tells them they are. This type of abuse will affect every aspect of the limbic system and will also cause deep fissure memories that are located in the unconscious and no-conscious parts of the brain. The resulting alter that is created will be a complete slave that is molded to the will of their abuser. They will have a complete state of helplessness and hopelessness and will actually be more afraid, of disappointing or losing their abuser than of getting free. The alternate identities have been created by the abusive situation. They have never experienced freedom nor a free will so they do not even have the ability to desire that which they need. What is worse, is that by the abuser, hurting and inflicting pain upon the alternate identity that identity becomes conditioned to receive pain, as pleasure and abuse as love. The pain and pleasure reward centers are linked and through the abuse they become reversed for the victim. The abused alter only feels loved, when it is being hurt or abused. This is why they do not seek freedom, nor independence; their identities have been created from abuse and that is where they find their self value. Unless someone that they care for is in danger of being hurt or they become convinced that they are going to be killed they will not seek help.

Conditions for the life essence

In order for the core life essence of the person to survive, it needs to be separated from the memories that the abused alternate identity possesses. To do this the brain creates a constant state of dissociative amnesia.

NOTE: The more abuse that the person endures the greater the barriers of amnesia that will be created.

The young woman that had came to me was suffering from an obsessive compulsive thought disorder in the form of continual thoughts of sexual gratification and also a compulsive obsessive disorder that was carried out by an inability to stop masturbating. These sexual obsessions were spilling over into other areas of her life. When she went to church she found that she was having uncontrollable sexual urges towards those in positions of leadership of the church and also the young girls in the church's religious school. What she did not know is that her abused alternate identity was evolving into a sexual predator. She was becoming just like the camp counselor! Even though she was constantly struggling with these urges; it was getting harder for her to control them. This is what led her to being referred to me for help.

Because the reward center of the brain is connected with the pleasure of eating and also sexual stimulation, a person with sexual problems will often have an eating disorder. This young ladies abuse had created an eating disorder. She began starving herself. Her alter had been trained to enjoy pain as pleasure and the pain and she told me that the experience of feeling her stomach hurting from being empty was incredibly joyful to her. When she came to me she was bordering on being anorexic. Her eating disorder was coupled with reoccurring and compulsive sexual fantasies that haunted her every night leading her into masturbation to try and satisfy the urges. The pleasure that she found in masturbation was very short lived. She began habitually masturbating, not only at night but she would go into the bathroom at the church where she worked to bring herself to climax. She found that she had to release herself several times throughout the day. These acts were resulting from the compulsive thoughts that were continually haunting her, day and night. This is called a obsessive compulsive thought disorder. It is because of an inner pain that is seeking to be released but cannot get free. The person is in need of catharsis. She said that the continual masturbation had caused her injury and that her body was unable to heal because she could not quit long enough for healing to occur. She knew these feelings were wrong and that they went against everything that her church taught, but she felt helpless and not keep herself from wanting to give in to them. What she did not know is that she had an alternate identity that did not have the ability to make its own decisions nor control its behavior.

Catharsis happens by releasing the pain of the alter and bringing healing

It was at this point in the therapy that she began to remember other incidents in her life. I sought to attach her mind with the alternate identities mind so she could see the memories of what she had been involved in. It was then that the memories began to come back to her, memories of what she had done with her body and what had been done to her. All of this had happened without conscious memory. She wanted to know why she had not remembered any of the incidents before but now they were so clear. The fears, the pain the sick feeling and the immense hatred all came back. What she had experienced, is described as dissociate amnesia.

Dissociate Amnesia

Dissociative Amnesia, which is also called *"psychogenic amnesia,"* is defined as inability to recall important person information. The mind does not have the ability to remember the information because it is too painful for the person to deal with. The brain separates the information through dissociation and then hides all of the details and events containing the stressful overload. It can be a situation involving trauma, abuse, neglect, or anything that is too stressful for the mind to deal with. It is called amnesia because the memories are still in the brain they just have been separated from the presenting identity. Dissociates will have some degree of amnesia. It is a major component of the disorder. Every alternate identity has a degree of dissociative amnesia. It is the amnesiac barriers that keep the segregation partitions between the alters intact. Any information that tries to cross between alters of varying roles will be absorbed into the amnesiac barrier surrounding the identities.

When working with someone I suspect of having DID I ask them about their childhood. It is very common for the dissociate to have very little memory of their childhood. Some will have no ability to remember any of their childhood. Take for an example a man I worked with, who was considered to be a genius in the field of his employment. When I asked him about his childhood he told me he had a terrible memory and could not remember any of his childhood, only tiny bits and pieces. So to test his memory I asked him questions about a former conversation we had several months before. I had taken notes on the meeting and to my surprise he was able to recite almost verbatim what we had discussed. This showed that he had an excellent memory. I asked him about world events and even specifics such as quotes found in various books. He was able to answer these questions almost effortlessly. This man had an incredibly advanced capacity for memory! The only area that I found, that he could not focus upon, was his childhood. I began to pressure him on areas of his childhood when he became angry. His voice changed. It became deeper and it switched from a New England accent to foreign dialect and accent. His body posture completely changed. The questioning caused the man to trigger and another alternate identity came forth. This alter was completely aware of his childhood and the challenging the man's memories caused it to switch places with him. When it came forth is was very angry over me trying to dig up his childhood memories. At the end of the session the man switched back having no recollection of what had transpired in the session. He even asked me when we were going to start. I recognized that this man was a high level dissociate so to better help him I asked for his permission to contact his sibling and parents, who were still living. He granted me that permission so that week I contacted his parents and siblings and they told me that his childhood had been incredibly abusive. His sibling said that he was regularly beaten and physically abused so badly, that often, they did not know how he lived through it! Also another area that later was uncovered was that he had been sexually abused by his mother while the father had been away, (the fathers work kept him on the road traveling most of the time). His mother had started having incest with him at the age of four, something that was still continuing over forty years later. This family was riddled with a great amount of incest that included his abusing his younger siblings from the age of twelve to just before his twentieth birthday. This man's life contained all the ingredients needed for DID; he was a complex dissociate.

While working with him I found no less than seven primary alters. Each of these alters were specialists in their respective field of employment and entertainment. Everyone of his primary alters had reached pinnacle points in their careers. A normal person would have to take a lifetime to achieve what just one of his alters had accomplished and he had seven primary alters that had all been very successful. All were in different, completely un-related fields. He had accomplished in several fields what would have taken a normal person a lifetime to achieve in just one. This man had mastered no less than two fields in the scientific world and at least four dealing with fine arts and one in high end extreme sports. He was recognized for his skills and was being professionally sought after. How was he able to do this? The trauma that caused his dissociated states had created several primary alternate personalities, that each focused independently on the specific field they were created for. In essence he had seven different, dominate and driven men all living inside of him and they all became the best in their respective fields of work. This takes a great deal of mental energy and memory retention!

To put him to the test, I asked him a question dealing with bio-physics, he instantly triggered and switched to an alter that knew about bio-physics, and without hesitation, answered the question. It was during this time I was working on my PhD. So I asked him a question relating to psychology and to my amazement he triggered and out came another alter that was a psychologist/psychiatrist. He not only answered my question but then told me which meds would work best under those conditions. I asked him if he ever had studied psychology and he said yes, but not technically, while in college. He said that when he sought to work his way into an executive position in a top company, he realized that his efforts were not going to get him the promotions he needed. It was then, that he began researching psychology, to better understand what it would take to achieve his goals. He studied psychology in his spare time, (to the point of doctorate level). After acquiring the knowledge and understanding, of the qualities that the executives in the firm were looking for, his brain created an alter that matched the skills and had a projected personality they were looking for. This alter oozed with confidence and was immediately given the position. In less than two years he had worked his way to being an executive in a top company in the region where he lived, making a salary that most individuals never dream of. This man had achieved success, through the adaptable ability of being, a high level dissociate.

The way the brain of a high end dissociate functions is as follows: If a primary alter has a goal to reach, but runs into a block, or something that keeps it from reaching its ultimate end, than the brain will research and analysis everything involving that goal, it will then do what must be done, in order to achieve the desired results. In this man's case, another alter was created that was tailored to fill the positional needed. All of the research and planning, to include the creation of another alter was done, in order to aid the engineering identity to reach its full potential. Now, why did I tell you all of this? It was to show that this man had no problems with his memory. What he did have was Dissociate Amnesia. As a matter of fact, he had selective memory. Selective memory is the ability to recall specific memories verbatim, whether seen, heard, read or spoken. Dissociative amnesia was the method that this man's brain chose to use in order to ensure his survival and personal developmental wellness.

A case study example

A young woman came to me having an unnatural hatred for her father. I asked her if he had ever done anything to make her feel such hatred for him and she said there was nothing she could think of. This was a very vibrant and beautiful Christian lady, who was carrying an enormous burden of guilt, over these lingering feelings of hatred that she had for him. As we began to explore the reasons why she may be feeling like this, she told me that she had this over powering impression in her mind, that he had molested and raped her, even though, she had no memories of anything that would suggest, he had ever been anything but the perfect father. We prayed and I asked the Lord to reveal the truth to her, as to why she would be so angry. The following is what ensued.

She said, "I see me in my father's hands as a child of about two years of age. He is taking *me* into the bathroom and he puts me on the sink. Next I see him taking my diaper off and then his head goes into my lap." [At this point a blank expression comes over her face and I can see that she is being triggered] "Go on," I say. "That's all. All I see, is him putting clothes on the little girl and she looks like she is crying." I asked her if she recognized the little girl and she said that she could not, but for some reason, it looked like she did, when she was a child.

NOTE: Not only did she having dissociate amnesia, but now that she was having to confront the issues that caused the amnesia, her mind had switched her perceptional ability of recall to that of being completely detached and depersonalized. This is a common, characteristic trait response mechanism that is a part of the identity coping system in those, who have suffered molestation from a parent or major caregiver.

Here is an example of selective amnesia. She was able to see the event leading up to the incident, and that which occurred after the incident, but had no recollection of the "in between time." "Many findings relate incest and other forms of childhood sexual abuse to psychogenic amnesia and other dissociate symptoms."[27]

---

[27] Betrayal Trauma, The logic of Forgetting Childhood Abuse, —Jennifer J. Freyd; Harvard University Press; Cambridge Massachusetts; 1996

Another form of dissociate amnesia is when it is localized. Localized amnesia often happens when a person is confronted with overwhelming tragedy. For instance, it is very common when a spouse has lost a loved one, that is very dear like their spouse or child and then they have no time for grieving. They have to prepare for the burial, notify everyone and then endure the procession of visitation, burial and then the bereavement meal. When everything is finally over it is a very common occurrence for them to be unable to recall any or most of the events of the week. This is because the string of events has been too overwhelming and traumatic. The brain dissociates the memories and applies amnesia to avoid further stress and trauma to the person. The type of dissociation is that of fugue.

Dissociative fugue

On the other end of the phone the young man was very upset and confused; "Tell me what is wrong," I asked. "I don't know where I am, I mean, I just woke up and I'm driving in some city and I don't know where I am! I don't know what to do!" The person I was speaking with had experienced a Dissociative Fugue episode. I had just began working with the young man we will call Joe and had instructed him call me whenever he found himself in a position like this. It was very traumatic for him, as he would wake up in cities sometimes several states away, not knowing how he got there or even why he was there. The solution was easy enough, I would pray and ask the Lord to reveal to him, why he was there and for what purpose. The Lord would calm him down and the appropriate alter would come to the surface and then everything would be in order. What was happening was that he would fugue while another identity in him that was the driver would take him to his destination, but the driver was being switched back down and he was coming back up in the wrong order. His parameters were melting down and it was causing his systems to run erratically.

Let me restate the problem fugue can create when it is out of order

This was not the first time Joe had called me with this problem. I found this case to be very sad, because this young man would often trigger and fugue while driving and when he would come back to an active state of conscious, he would not know where he was or even how he had gotten there. It was a very dramatic and terrifying ordeal for him. It did not help that he was terrible at driving, averaging at least one accident a year. Because of his lack of driving skills he would avoid going to any large cities or areas he was unfamiliar with. When he did have to go into a large city or unfamiliar area he would trigger and fugue and would wake up at his destination point, terrified and afraid. What he did not know was that he had an alter inside that was called, "the driver," and it was a very skilled driver. The driver was very professional. It had been certified in defensive driving courses and had been used to high ranking officials while he was in the military. But this man was completely unaware of the driver. When he would fugue he would wake up, sometimes days later in another part of the country, not realizing that he had driven there for work, and the result would be confusion and fear.

When the episodes first began the client was unaware of the fugue episodes happening. He would wake up near his destination and would think that he had been falling asleep at the wheel and would be amazed that he could have driven such a long distance without any accident. I asked him how he had gotten to his destination and he explained it to me like this, "I must have fallen asleep. I was in …. And then I wake up in ….. How could I have driven over 12-15 miles asleep though?"

He was not falling asleep. He was experiencing a fugue episode. I challenged his denial system and the scripts[28] that were running with the truth. That there was no legitimate way a person could drive 12 to 15 miles while asleep with no accident, especially since he would have had to stop at traffic lights, cross railroad tracks and make turns. I did this in order to make him question the validity of what he believed to be true. He came to me because he thought he had a sleep disorder. He thought he was falling asleep at the wheel. He had no idea that he was a dissociate. I had to help him to realize what was really happening.

NOTE: The first step to bringing a person to healing is to confront them with the truth and to make them aware of what they are doing.

In this man's case he would fugue while driving because of triggers that were being set off but also from environmental cueing. This is what caused his internal systems to malfunction. Once the triggering began he would immediately dissociate with several other alters rising to the surface, all at the same time. One of these alters was a young child alter that would be confused and terrified because it did not know where it was or why it was there. The child alter when triggered came to the first layer of the conscious, the problem was that instead of going all the way back down to the un-conscious it was staying in the second and third layer of the conscious so when the man came back into the first layer of consciousness, he would

---

[28] Scripts are pre-planned explanations that the brain tells the mind happened in order to prevent the person from knowing the truth about their condition.

emphatically feel and experience all the confusion and terror of the child alter, but not knowing why. During this fugue episode he was unconscious of driving the vehicle, only when the fugue episode ceased, would he once again become aware of his surroundings.

As I sought to find the root issues, causing the dissociative patterns, I found that his episode patterns originated from being in a vehicle while driving around specific locations. This is called *environmental cueing*. Environmental cueing is a specific set of triggers associated with trauma, that has happened in a set region or location. If a person has been repeatedly traumatized or abused in a specific setting, they will associate the abuse with the immediate environment where the abuse took place. By returning to the location of the abuse, the mind will re-initiate the dissociate episode, of whatever type, the child's mind has previously used. Let me give you an illustration of the various components of environmental cueing:

A middle aged woman came to see me with unexplained bouts of rage, anger and bitterness, which would rise up within her for no apparent reason. These bouts of emotion would leave her feeling drained and depressed, for several hours each time they happened. This emotional seesaw began interfering with her marriage and ability, to be a wife and mother. Her husband had taken her to see several different mental health specialists and they could find no apparent reason for the emotional surges so they did put her on several different medications to suppress the feelings. The medications did not stop the emotional outbursts; they exacerbated the problem by making her feel drugged. This was taking a toll on her and was causing problems with her husband and children. I began by asking her a serious of questions in order to find the root of the problem, when out of nowhere, the woman triggered and switched to a young teenage alter. I did not expect this. I honestly did not suspect she was DID. I found that the woman's emotional problems were stemming from being a simple dissociate. She had been sexually and physically abused as a child by her father. The emotional imbalances that she was experiencing were the result of several internal alters being triggered and rising to the subconscious. Their emotions became her emotions. She was unaware of the other alters within her and did not have any knowledge or memory of the abuse that had happened. This is why she would feel this overwhelming flood of emotions come over her, for no apparent reason. I talked with the different alters, and lead to release the anger and bitterness, asking the Lord to forgive her father and to heal the alters before asking the Lord to integrate them back into the woman. The alters told me that when the woman was four years old, her mother had gotten switched to third shift where she worked. It was after this that the father began coming into her room, where he would molest her with pencils and other objects. This molestation happened into her teen years, progressing to the point where he would force her to take showers in front of him and then do, perverted acts for him. He liked to watch her perform before ending each night with him forcing himself upon her sexually, sodomizing her. The first time he had molested her she had begun bleeding from her genital area so the father made her pull all the bedding off of her bed and then had her carry them down stairs to the laundry room where he taught her to wash and dry her bedding before putting it back on her bed. She was not able to go to bed at night until she had taken a shower and then washed and replaced all of her bedding. I found out during the session that the woman had four different installed on the bathroom door because she had this fear that someone would walk into the bathroom while she was showering. This woman had gotten married later in life, in her mid thirties, because her father had continued to use her for himself until his wife quit working. So here she was in her mid thirties with two small children that were four and six years of age. What I found interesting about this case was that the emotional bouts did not begin until after her youngest child had turned four years of age. The first time she triggered was when she was washing the child's undergarments and bedding. For some reason it triggered her memories of when she had been traumatized by her father and had to wash her own bedding and clothing. I believe the cause of this was that her youngest son looked just like her and she was seeing herself in him. The pain that had been locked away for so many years in those young alters was now rising to the subconscious affecting her with emotional over load. Here were the environmental cueing triggers associated with the alters inside of this woman.

1) Sound-
   a. When the woman would hear her mother go out of the house and get into her car she would begin to dissociate

b. The alter knew it needed to get ready to do its job when it would hear its father walking up the stairs. It had counted the steps up the stairs.

c. Smell-This alter hated the smell of blood and feces. She would not eat meat as a result of not being able to stand the sight of blood. She associated these two smells with being molested and abused.

2) Pressure on top of her-She could not bear having anyone on top of her because of this her husband could not perform any sexual relations with her unless she was on top. The first time he tried to make love to her she screamed and kicked him off the bed.

3) Sight-

a. When she saw a shower she was terrified that someone would come into the bathroom and would see her naked.

b. Children's bedding and undergarments. When she had to wash them it triggered her, bringing out all of the pain and fear that had laid dormant for nearly two decades.

c. Her child's fourth birthday. When her child turned four it brought up memories about, how after she turned four years of age her life changed into one long drawn out form of ritual abuse.

The Lord brought all of the woman's alters to healing and integration so that she was able to be a good wife and mother, without overwhelming fear or emotional trauma. She actually began living life with freedom and joy. She is off all of the medications and no longer suffers from emotional surges of any kind.

When abuse has happened in a specific location, the abused person will instantly trigger and switch to the abused alternate identity when they encounter the abuser in or near that location. The process of fugue episodes will become instantaneous and autonomic. A person that has been through repetitive bouts of trauma, where dissociate fugue has been the primary method of escape, will develop the ability, to instantly dissociate through fugue episode, from any trauma or extreme stress. Fugue will become the preferred method of dealing with all future stressors. The man that would fugue will driving, had experienced abuse in many different locations, where he had grown up as a child. The common denominator to the various locations of abuse was it had always happened while being in a vehicle. Because his life had become too complicated, the integrity of his systems was being compromised, resulting in an inability to completely switch his internal alters, leaving him disorientated and confused. His systems had become over taxed. What worsened his situation was that his triggering system was on overdrive, combining elements from several different alters. This caused alter at once to be triggered. The control mechanism would become confused over which alter should be top so rather than putting the wrong alter into the conscious position it would leave them in the 2nd and 3rd layer of the conscious, and then bring him out of fugue to experience putting him back into the seat of active consciousness. Because the other alters were in the 2nd and 3rd layers of the sub and anterior conscious, all their emotions were felt and experienced by him. He would come out of fugue, disorientated, confused and over ridden with a surge of powerful emotions. The following are some of the triggers that would set the switching process into order while he was driving.

- ☐ A song on the radio
- ☐ A passing object
- ☐ A evoked memory
- ☐ Driving (often he would be abused on trips)
- ☐ A familiar land object

What had happened in his case, was that his father would often become enraged while driving. Many of these times the father would be drinking alcohol and driving, when the fits of rage would come over him. For the man, the abuse began while he was a very young child, [pre-adolescent]. He would be seated in the front seat, between the father and mother and when the rage would overtake his father, he would begin to beat the boy's mother, while he was driving. The mother would be screaming and begging him to stop but he would continue to swinging his fist over the young child's body striking the mother in the face and chest and often times pulling her hair, dragging her over the young child, and beating her while her body was covering the strapped in child. This caused him to begin dissociating. The toddler would often try to cover the mother with his hands but this only provoked the father to attack him as well. As the child grew older, he was placed in the back seat of the car but this did not stop the abuse. When the father would go into a rage and begin beating the mother, the young boy would yell for the father to stop and this would cause the father to turn in his seat while driving and then slap the child in the face several times. Sometime the father would pull the car over to the side of the road where he would jump out and grab the young boy, dragging him out of the car by his head, arm or leg and then would beat him in the ditch. The father would use his fists and feet. There were times when he almost would kick the boy to death. The only escape for this young man had been, to instantly dissociate whenever the father would go into a rage; this was how he escaped the traumatic abuse.

Fugue had become such a common part of this man's life that he commonly would often wake up in strange areas, not knowing why he was there. What I found particularly interesting, is that, his fugue episodes began after he moved back to his home town. When he had to move to another part of the state for employment the fugue episodes stopped. Was it because he ceased to be able to have fugue episodes? No, the ability to fugue was still there but the triggers associated with the abuse, were only associated with the landmarks of his home town so once he moved to the new area; the fugue episodes stopped. The fugue episode triggers were from a combination of landscape and scenery coupled with driving. I suspect that if he were to move back to his old home town that the fugue episodes would begin reoccurring. Once fugue episode triggers have been established they will remain in place until the memories and trauma are properly dealt with and the conscious has been brought to healing. Unless the source of trauma that caused the initial fugue episodes is removed, the potential for having more fugue episodes will always present. A fugue episode is identified by the primary characteristic which is ***having a loss of time***. I have spoken with many dissociates who fugue on a regular basis.

The different types of dissociation, all share a similar function; they are a part of the human response, to stress and memory. Tests have revealed that those who have Dissociative fugue episodes will also score high in Dissociative capacity, along with the ability to be easily hypnotized. Some therapists believe that fugue episodes are closely related to childhood self-hypnosis, a method employed to escape extreme duress situations. It is my opinion that fugue does not stem from self hypnosis but is an affect that rises from the cueing of former trauma.

As in operand conditioning, the survivor of multiple assaults will develop an internal system that produces optimum results in protecting the mind of the victim. The mind always seeks a way to escape, having to deal with the pain of the trauma, thus it creates a series of amnesiac barriers that constantly have to be maintained. Fugue is one method of accomplishing that goal, by distancing the person from the triggers and memories that may potentially, through remembrance, re-traumatize the person. It is important to understand, that individuals with Dissociative conditions do not have poor memories, actually the opposite is true, they have incredibly vivid and detailed memories. When a dissociate remembers a traumatic event, the more painful that event has been, the more real and detailed will be their remembrance of the event. Memories, for the dissociate are not just a flash of words or a few pictures that come into their minds. Dissociates often have full body memories, where they relive the event or trauma. The memory will be so intense, that it will feel as if the trauma is happening to them, right there and then. Bruises and cuts will reappear on their bodies. They will physically hurt; they will smell aromas that were present during the time of the trauma. All of the emotions that they felt during those moments, will come rushing back like a tidal wave, flooding over their entire being. That is why it is called flooding.

NOTE: Flooding is when the memories of an alter, that has suffered abuse or trauma are released into the conscious mind. Because of the amount of energy that has been used to keep the memories separated from the active conscious, when the memories do break loose, they flood the mind and body with emotion, visual, perceptional and auditory memories. The experience completely overwhelms the individual.

Let me restate this for emphasis: When a dissociate remembers a traumatic event, it is as if they are there re-living the even all over again. The dissociate mind not only remembers the event, but so does their body. Old wounds and bruises can reappear. If they have been disciplined, by specific wound types, like having their fingers or other appendages given small cuts similar to those resulting from a paper cut, then when the alter with those wounds rises to the second or third layer of the conscious, the cuts will reappear. It is common for ritual abuse victims that have had this type of discipline to wake up in the morning with small paper cuts on their fingers not knowing how the cuts got there. This is a part of neural body memories. When a dissociate floods, all of the emotions that have been hidden away, in the recesses of the unconscious and no-conscious parts of the brain, will suddenly come back, along with the fear and pain. This is why the mind, in order to survive will sever the connection of the pain from the person.

> **I M P O R T A N T**
>
> *Remember when the dissociates amnesiac barriers weaken, and their memories began to return, the memories will be so vivid and real, that the effect will be as if they are re-experiencing the horrific act or event.*

When flooding does occur, it causes further dissociation, reinforcing the boundaries that were once established from the initial split of the conscious. This will also increase the depression, fear, and hyper-vigilance associated within the isolated alters. My personal thoughts on fugue are; Fugue is an act that is used for knowledge isolation and protective psyche management. Freyd speaks on the subject of knowledge isolation, in the book, "Betrayal Trauma."

Living with constant reoccurring traumatic memories would make life unbearable, keeping the person's mind and emotions in a constant state of upheaval and re-settling. For this cause, dissociative fugue episodes are often a blessing, as they give the person the ability to contain the memories with amnesiac barriers until they can be dealt with in a holistically healthy manner. The goal in counseling is to bring healing and restoration to the client, not to re-traumatize them. This is one of the many negative aspects of the theophostic approach to counseling. It has a tendency to re-traumatize the victim, causing further dissociation.

Dissociative Identity Disorder

I was approached by a married couple with the wife asking me if I could make time in my schedule to speak with her about their marriage, so we went into my office while her husband waited outside the door. As we sat down, I asked her if it would be ok for us to pray before we started the session. After I finished praying, I lifted up my head and noticed her body was repositioned in a manner, like that of a man, rather than a lady. (She was wearing a short dress and the way that she was sitting was open legged, revealing herself). I asked her what it was that she would like to discuss and to my surprise her speech and mannerisms were definitely not of a woman's. The person sitting in front of me had switched from the female church member that I knew into a rough spoken man. During the prayer she had triggered and switched into an alternate personality. The alter sitting in front of me was a man, who was the protector of the woman's body and also was the Guardian over her internal systems. He/she opened the conversation by telling me that since I was her pastor, I needed to talk with her husband, because he, (this male alter), was getting fed up with the way the husband was treating the wife. (He was actually the wife, but he spoke of her in the third person).

NOTE: When a person has complete dissociate identity disorder they will have alters that are completely developed with their own thoughts, agendas, personalities, and roles, that they perform. The integrity of the alternate identity is so fully developed that when they see themselves in mirrors, the alternate identity will see themselves, as they believe that they appear to be. This is distorted image perception and a part of the denial system within the dissociate.

I worked with a small 5'2" woman that weighed less than 100 pounds but she had a wardrobe in her closet for a 300 pound man complete with shoes and undergarments. When she looked into the closet she did not see his clothing, which was hanging on one side of the closet with hers on the other. This is also a part of the denial system, she could be looking directly at the other alters belongings and not be able to see them or even know they were there. If she touched them she would not feel them. She had two primary alters; she was the first and she would be out during the day and he was the second primary alter and he came out at night. When her alters switched places at night, she would go to sleep in her bed, (this was her script) and he would get out of bed, (his script was that he had just woken up from sleeping all day) and he would dress the body with his clothes. He/she would wear his cloths and he would perform his role as the man until the middle of the night when he would literally go back to bed and they would both sleep until morning. She would wake up as this petite woman, who would get up and go about her day. She was a dissociate with two complete identities.

When a person dissociates and switches alters, they will take on all of the mannerisms and customs of the complete alter. I worked with a man that weighed over three hundred pounds, was middle aged and had brown hair but in his mind he was in perfect, athletic shape, with blond hair and he believed that all woman adored and wanted his body. When that alter would rise to the surface it would strut and prate in front of others saying, "Go ahead and take it all in, you deserve some eye candy." They could look but not touch. I had to confront his denial system so one day I had a mirror prepared and asked him to look into it and to tell me what he saw. I watched as he smiled when he saw himself in the mirror. He was really admiring himself. He could not hide the conceit . When he would look into a mirror he saw chiseled abs, muscled arms and bright blond hair but in reality he was obese, flabby and had thinning brown hair. I even reached out and took ahold of a layer of his fat that was hanging down around his mid section and told him to grab it and tell me what it was. He said, "What are you talking about? You don't get abs like this from sitting around. I've worked hard to keep this body." He then rubbed his stomach like it was rock hard.

The denial system creates a mental psychosis that projects the image of what the alter, *believes it looks like*, not what it really is. In the case with the woman, who had asked to speak to me, when she switched to the male alter that was sitting in front of me, he fully believed in his mind that he was a rough and tough construction worker, that could get very violent if he needed to. He began telling me about things that the husband expected her to do for him. There were many sexual demands that that he imposed on her that she did not like to do. The husband was also expecting too much from her with all of the household chores. She worked a full time job and also had to do all of the work at the house for him and their children and then cater to all of his physical and sexual needs every night, which were sometimes quite physically demanding, being drawn out for long periods of time. All of this was upsetting the wife. She was tired and wanted to go to bed but did not have the will to say no. He said that he was getting tired of the way she was being treated and if it did not change, quickly, he was going to have to do something about it. He told me that just the following week that he had gotten angry with the husband and had grabbed him by the shirt and slammed him up against the wall, lifting him off of his feet and holding him in the air, against the wall. (Understand this woman was thin and petite and the husband was easily a hundred pounds heavier than her. I later confirmed from her husband that this had actually happened and he was afraid that he might provoke her again. He shared with me that it upset him to the point where he was considering filing for divorce. This male alter, whose role was that of the protector inside of the woman, proceeded to tell me that the wife did not want a divorce but that he personally thought she should get one, saying, "the guy is a jerk off." He said that he had been trying to get her to divorce him but she would not listen to him. He also informed me that the next time this guy made her cry he was going to beat the living h… out of him and I believed him!

Thankfully, we were able to work through their problems and today the family is still together and happy. The husband never found out that his wife had Dissociate Identity Disorder. She has been brought to healing, and though she still has eight alters, with primary and secondary roles, she is functioning quite well.

Dissociates can function very well in society

I have been asked many times how a person can have multiple alters and actively function in society and the answer is quite simple, it is the many alters, that enable the person to interact in society. Many will ask, "How can this be possible." Some have seen the movie "Sybil" where the main character was a complex Dissociate with over a dozen primary alters. Each of her alters had their own identities and played a specific role in her life. It is the multiplicity that equips and enables the dissociate to live, a seemingly normal life, in front of others, while secretly harboring the pain and brokenness that results from ritual abuse and/or trauma. The ability to dissociate and create identities, that are tailored made for specific roles, is the epitome of hypocrisy, but it is also, the only way that these abused victim, can psychologically survive events that are unbearable and often unimaginable, while still having to function and openly interface, in the society and culture they are a part of.

DID is the disorder formerly referred to as Multiple Personality Disorder. There have been several movies in the past depicting this fascinating ability, in which an individual can actually have several, distinctly different alters within them. Each of these alters will have their own likes, dislikes, desires etc. They will possess character and personality traits that are theirs alone. There is an incredible individuality and

114

uniqueness that makes each alter what it is. In cases of poly-fragmentation there can be several shades of varying degrees of difference from a specific alter. For instance, I have found individuals, that have had a dozen alters named Dorothy. These were quadrinary splits. Each of these Dorothy's looked the same and acted the same but in reality they all had subtle changes in their mindsets, character and abilities. Dorothy #1 was a totally different person than Dorothy #12. Dorothy #1 was an innocent girl wanting someone to help her find her way home while Dorothy # 12 was a wicked witch, whose home was in the fantasy world created inside the persons mind. Dorothy # 1 was dependant and desirous for the help of others but Dorothy # 12 was very independent, evil and actively practiced witchcraft against everyone in the whole person's life.

In DID the varying alters will possess a great deal of diversity. The dissociate can have an alter that likes Italian food but at the same time have an alter that hates Italian food. They may have an alter that has a specific medical problem, like diabetes, and another that does not have the disease, yet they share the same body. Because the mind and body work in conjunction, whatever the mind believes to be true, becomes true for the body. This is why it is possible, that the alters can have many different medical conditions that are unique to a particular alternate identity. I have seen alters that needed strong eye glasses in order to see while another, in the same body, had perfect 20/20 vision. These physiological control mechanisms are somatically controlled and are a part of the neural-linguistic programming, associated within each independent alter. The individual uniqueness of the dissociated alter, is not limited to physical conditions and their personal tastes, but also includes their intelligence. A person may have an identity that is a master of the English language, while also having another alter that cannot even read its own name. The unique individuality of alters, also includes age factoring. I have found dissociate that possess alters that are children and also have other alters that are elderly. They can have individual alternate identities that span all five of the life cycles, in the same body. This is a phenomenon that shows the power and influence that the mind can have over the body.

I have personally worked with individuals, who have had several thousand alters within them. This is called poly-fragmentation. Poly-fragmentation is a condition where an alternate identity is further split into other alternate identities. The following is a list of splitting potential.

    I.   The First split created two primary alters. They will divide the left and right hemisphere of the brain but will be attached to the opposite side. They will regulate the influence that the other hemisphere has on themselves and further splits

       a. Primary One-Left Hemiosphere

       b. Primary Two-Right Hemisphere

    II. Each of the Primaries can be split into two creating four primaries alternate identities in all.

       a. Primary One

          i. Primary One A-Left Hemisphere

         ii. Primary One B-Left Hemisphere

    b. Primary Two-Right Hemisphere

        i. Primary Two A-Right Hemisphere

        ii. Primary Two B-Right Hemisphere

III. Each of these Four Primaries can be split into two to six secondary alternate identities. They will all be variations of the Primary they are split out of.

    a. Primary One

        i. Primary One A-Left Hemisphere

            1. Secondary A-Left Hemisphere

            2. Secondary B-Left Hemisphere

            3. Secondary C-Left Hemisphere

NOTE: In mind control programming these three secondary alters in females will often be named a variation of; the mother, the maiden and the krone. In male's they will be called; the father, the son and the grandfather.

        ii. Primary One B-Left Hemisphere

            1. Secondary A-Left Hemisphere

            2. Secondary B-Left Hemisphere

            3. Secondary C-Left Hemisphere

    b. Primary Two-Right Hemisphere

        i. Primary Two A-Right Hemisphere

            1. Secondary A-Right Hemisphere

            2. Secondary B-Right Hemisphere

            3. Secondary C-Right Hemisphere

        ii. Primary Two B-Right Hemisphere

1. Secondary A-Right Hemisphere
2. Secondary B-Right Hemisphere
3. Secondary C-Right Hemisphere

Out of each of the secondary splits can be split an additional 1 to 3 trilinary alternate identities and out of each of the trilinaries can be split an additional 12 alternate identities. There is a balance within the structure of the alternate systems. It is designed like a set of weights and counter weights keeping everything in a state of balance. For every evil alter there will be a good alter. The more given over to evil the one alter is the more devoted to good will be the opposite. When this design is created it is referred to as *the kaleidoscope,* as it creates a convergence point from which an unlimited number of alternate identities can be created. The trained mind can and will create a hybrid to meet the immediate presented need. Here is a diagram:

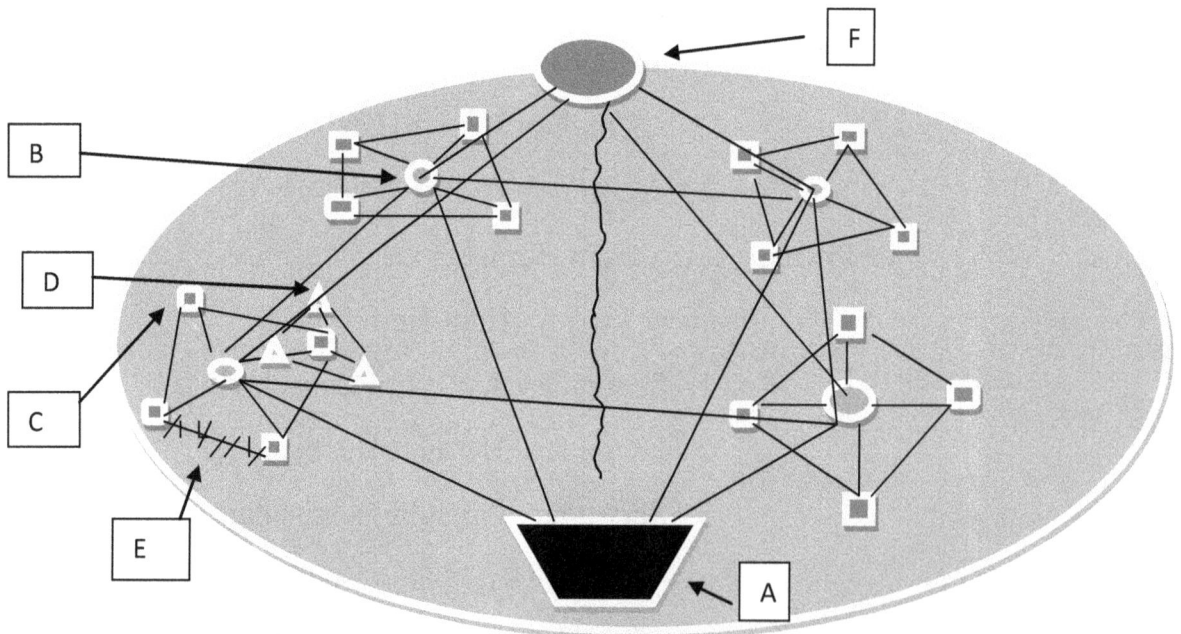

A = The brain stem. This is where the life essence erupts from passing into the brain.

B = A first Primary Split.

C = A Secondary split

D = A Trilinary split

E = The multiple Quadrinary splits

F = The active conscious where the presenting alter will be situated

Each of the alternate identities is a facet on the brain, which is the whole gem. The life force emitting from the brain stem, can mix the individual, secondary through quardrinay alternate identities, this creates a hybrid alternate identity with scattered memories, making it nearly impossible for complete memories to ever be recalled. This is the internal kaleidoscope.

When a person has begun dissociating in the infancy of life, they will have not had the ability nor the time frame needed to develop a personal identity. The life essence is split before it has time to get a proper foundation. What happens is that each of the primary alternate personalities created their own foundation, or world, with their own personal identity. They will have values and beliefs that are uniquely assigned to them only. All of the fragments in their world will share the same belief systems and life values. It is this type of development that allows for a person to be used as a mind control slave, without their ever knowing it. They will not have any idea that they are being used for anything. They will live life to the fullest in their own world while the other identities are doing the same.

At this point, I would like to take a moment to explain a bit more on the structure of how the psyche splits. The original splits are called primaries. When primaries are split the result is a secondary alter. The secondary alters can be further split, sequentially, into tri-linary alters which can be then also be split creating quadrinary alters. Quadrinay alters that are split are not able to become complete alternate identities. Splits from quardinraies are called shades. Shades are housing units that are like a shadow of the quadrinary alter. They are simple a detached aspect of a quadrinary alternate identity. Below is a simple diagram of a person that had been used sexually and as a result experienced a complete chain of splits.

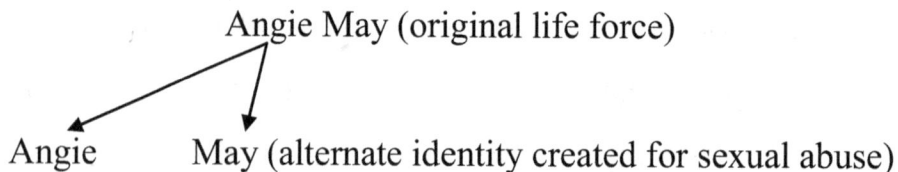

Angie May (original life force)

Angie   May (alternate identity created for sexual abuse)

Angie is the dissociated alter in state of fugue with amnesiac barriers preventing her from knowing about the sexual abuse that May endures. The psyche has split the mind into two separate identities that will develop individually from this point forward.

May (begins suffering ritual abuse)

The abuser begins using her for different purposes. Having her do different jobs for other individuals. This splits her into two secondary alters;

one that will be used by the original abuser and a second that is to perform for whoever he chooses:

May#1   May#2

May # 1 becomes a dominatrix and uses the alters of May # 2 to do what ever it needs to. She visualizes her world as a farm where the owner is her abuser and she keeps all of the animals in their respective pens until they need to be brought out and used. This happens because May's abuser wants to begin using her for bestiality so she splits into five trilinary alternate identities. Each one thinks it is a specific animal. By the alter being an animal there is no conflict within the inner mind when it performs its role. It is natural for animals to have sex with their own kind.

May# 2 splits into:
1) Prancer – a brown horse for sex with horses
2) Rosie – a dog for having sex with dogs
3) Emily- a pig for sex with pigs and also eats feces and drinks urine or spit
4) Dancer- a cat that will have sex with men or animals
5) Angel- that is also a horse but can become any of the other animals

In dissociation the life essence will be original energy that all the other alternate identities have been split from. The base of the life essence will be located in the deepest part of the no-conscious part of the brain. This is the top of the brain stem.

Splits occur when trauma surpasses the threshold barrier capacity of the life essence of the brain. Splits continue to occur anytime this barrier is surpassed in any of the alters until it becomes only shades or fragmented memories. The structure begins taking a permanent form after two primaries have been created. From there is continues spreading out and growing like the limbs of a tree. The first two primary alters will be located at the very base of the no-conscious of the brain just above the brain stem. This is the seventh layer of the conscious. The second two primaries will be located just above and forward of the original two in the sixth layer of the no-conscious. From these four points in the left and right hemisphere the secondary alters will begin growing up and out. When trauma has crossed the anterior threshold barrier of a secondary alter, it will split the conscious of the secondary alter creating two new alters. These are both called tri-linary alternate identities. These two new alters will be housed further down in the brain, away from the active conscious. The trilinary alters will tend to be close to the center of the brain above and just off to the sides of the brain stem. These will be the alters that show the three aspects of life, often called the mother, the maiden and the krone. If the trauma persists, the tri-linary alters will re-direct it back to one of the four secondary alters initiating a split that is called a quadrinary alternate identity. Quardrinary alters are shades of the secondary alter. They will be housed in the fifth layer of the brain which is the upper layer of the no-conscious. They will lie just beneath the fourth layer of the un-conscious. The no-conscious part of the brain is layer seven through five. This is the area that hypnotists communicate with when controlling a subject.

The more life essence a split has, the further away they will be stored away from the active conscious. A primary will be just above the life essence. A quadrinary will be just below the un-conscious layers of the brain. This is the how the psyche is structured. It begins in the top of the brain stem, where the formation of the identity is first located and then splits into separate foundations from that point on. It is the foundation of the identities psyche that their personal schema will be created. It is the bases and foundation for the entire identity structure. This is where neural linguistic programming is stored, in the identities foundation schema. Below is a graph to better illustrate the gradual depth of the alter staging.

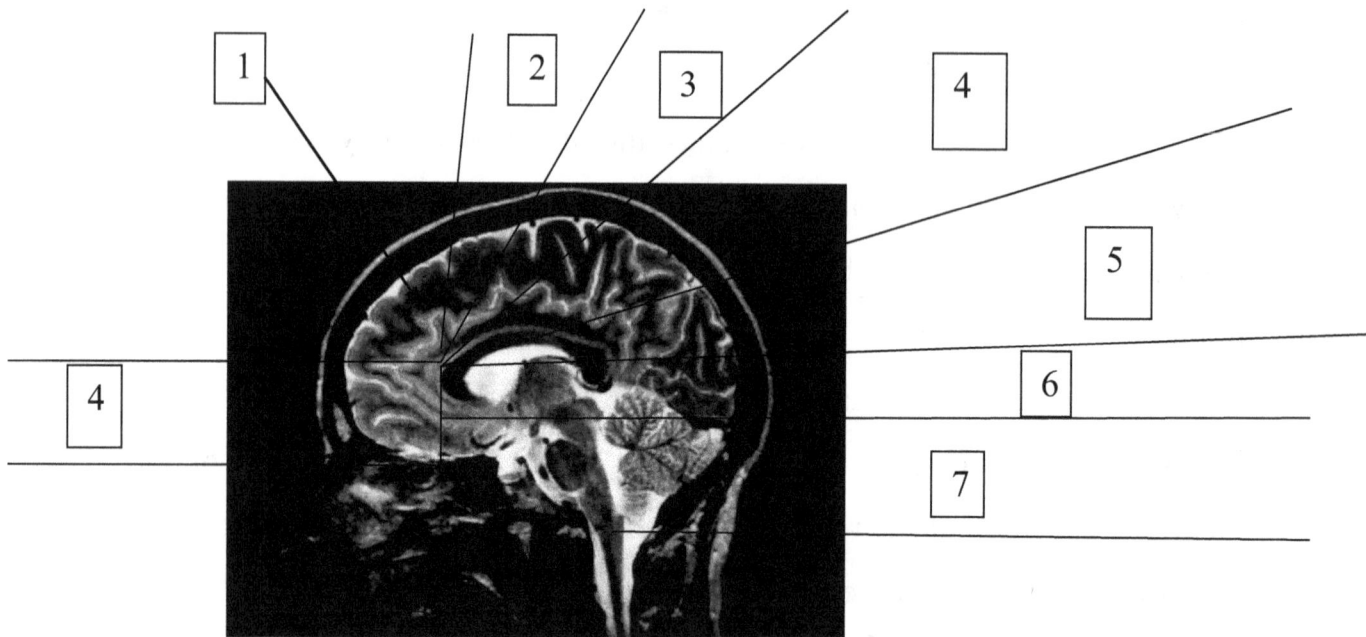

1) The Active Conscious

2) The Sub-conscious

3) The Anterior Aspect of the Sub-conscious

4) The Unconscious

5) The Dividing Barrier

6) The No-conscious

7) The Base Foundation

There are several factors that, when combined, cause poly-fragmentation.

1) The amount of trauma; it has to be a great deal of stress, both mental and physical. It can arise from fear, pain, electronic stimulation, etc.

2) The length of time that the stress is endured; if the trauma happens several times, over a period of several hours, and the person is given short breaks from the trauma/stress or torture this will give the alternate identity time to gather its composure and to solidify. When the trauma begins again, once the anterior threshold is surpassed the alter will split again, dissociating and driving the active conscious into a deeper layer of the brain in order to try and hide it from the stress. The more times it happens, the greater the amount of splits that will be created. The first splits will have the most potential for complete identity control. The last splits are discarded. They are only created as a byproduct of having to reinforce the trauma for solidifying the necessary alternate identities.

3) The setting must be one of hopelessness and helplessness. For instance, if the abused child knows the parents are there but are not stopping the trauma/torture but are actually a part of the abuse than it will create a state of helplessness and hopelessness. This is the mental fabric needed for poly-fragmentation. For this reason the parents and grandparents are a part of the dissociation of a monarch mind control slave.

4) In poly-fragmentation the brain will create many shell alters. A shell alter is one that is hollow. A shell alter has neither feelings nor emotions. Shells are empty storage points that can be used by the brain to create a new identity when needed. Since they are already created by stress/trauma the brain does not need to be re-traumatized

to create a new alter it will use a shell. This is the essence of the kaleidoscope. It can pull up a shell alter and mix any combination of alters in the matrix making a new alter whenever it needs to that can fit the profile that is needed at any time. In mind control slaves they will have periods where they re-traumatize the person so that they can refill the oasis with shell alters.

NOTE: The brain will hold the extra shell alters in two storage points called, the oasis. There are two oasis areas in the brain.

Once poly-fragmentation has happened these alter will be replacements for any alternate identities that are brought to healing and integrated. The deep tissue scaring of memories that happens during times of trauma/torture causes an ability to reproduce any alters that are removed and to down load the needed memories and information into a shell replacing the lost alternate identity. This is called cloning. Until all of the original memories, along with the negative energy and the scaring are removed, the brain will be able pull up one of the shell alters from the oasis, down load all the necessary memories and information that the clone needs and then stage it back into the matrix so that it will be there when it is time to perform its necessary role. This is a part of the survival coping system technique.

There is a confusion that counselors, psychologist, and psychiatrists experience, when working with the alternate identities in complex dissociates. This confusion is from a lack of understanding the differences between, primary, secondary, trilenary, quidrinary altars, fragments, and shades. All of these will all be discussed in further detail in chapter five.

The next book delves much deeper into the mind and dissociation. It is written primarily for counselors and lay people. People with DID live in a world filled with a great amount of emotional disturbance. One identifying trait is black and white thinking patterns. Dissociates deal with life in a driven and logical manner. They often do not possess the ability to interact well with others well for long periods of time. The next type of dissociation that will be covered is ***Depersonalization Disorder***. This is the end of Book I of the Big Book on Dissociate Identity Disorder the rest is continued in Book II. May the Lord richly bless you in all of your endeavors to serve Him. In Christ's love: Dr. Knotts, Jr.

www.ingramcontent.com/pod-product-compliance
Lightning Source LLC
Chambersburg PA
CBHW081418270326
41931CB00015B/3315